VALUE-ADDED CHRISTIANITY

BY THE SAME AUTHOR

"WALKING ON THE INSIDE - Strategies for Developing Life in His Presence"

VALUE-ADDED CHRISTIANITY

Putting Substance into
Reconsecration

COLIN CRAGO D. MIN.

Library of Congress Control Number: 2019900183
ISBN: Hardcover   978-1-9845-0489-0
                 Softcover   978-1-9845-0488-3
                 eBook   978-1-9845-0487-6

Print information available on the last page.

Rev. date: 02/15/2019

To order additional copies of this book, contact:
Xlibris
1-800-455-039
www.Xlibris.com.au
Orders@Xlibris.com.au
789953

CONTENTS

For 50 years of ministry people have advertently or inadvertently contributed to the text to this book. To all I give a hearty thanks, you have enriched my life. But, from childhood on, some pastors have made especial contributions. To these men, some of whom have passed on to their eternal reward, I dedicate this volume with great thanks for their perseverance with a somewhat recalcitrant subject.

G. T. FITZGERALD

J. E WEBB

R. B. EWERS

Clark TAYLOR

INTRODUCTION

Once upon a time, at the end of a crusade or a church Gospel meeting, the only people standing at the front of the meeting would be those declaring their allegiance to Christ for the first time. Now, in this twenty first century, most people who have journeyed from their seat to the front of the meting are those who have been there before. Evangelists are even looking for them in their appeals.

What is happening to these people?

In many cases they just go back to their seat to do whatever they were doing before the "new" pledge. In some cases they are reintroduced to a New Christian's Course teaching the basic doctrines of the faith. Some, in their enthusiasm to do what they think God wants, become victims of a cult. There seems little around specifically directed to those now hungry to go on with Jesus their saviour.

For many others reconsecration is a regular feature of their spiritual life as they attempt to live a life honouring Jesus.

"Epiphany" in the word used to describe the special vibrant, visionary revelational touch of God. Many of us do not get dramatic epiphanies but we do get special sensations of the Spirit of God stirring us. Maybe there is in it motivation to do something special but more likely it is a call from the Spirit to come closer to Jesus – special things may develop gradually at a later date.

The sense of God calling, even if it is just a whisper, should not be ignored. This could be a delightful opportunity for the aspirant to begin discovering the joy of being the type of disciple Jesus always wanted, sharing a positive relationship with Father, Son and Holy Spirit forever. This ought to be a time where "being" becomes more important than external stimuli. A time where the unique, creative influence of the individual, at the behest of the Spirit of God comes to the fore, fulfilling the role in the Body of Christ as only he/she uniquely can. In this age of instant everything it is necessary to realise that there is no such thing as instant disciples. Christian television programmes, daily devotionals etc are all trying to do the work for us. Excessive reliance on these things often put us in a place of second hand religion – needing someone else to do it for us. Such programmes are not wrong but they too-often fill a particular priestly role taking away a personal developing relationship with Jesus instead of adding to it.

Becoming what Jesus wants takes spiritual work!

This is certainly not a book offering you information about the latest ecclesiastical fad. It's not about theology or Old and New Testament histories and geography, nor is not about church polity or denominational allegiance, as important as all of these things are. It is trying to put you in a position where you can help yourself to grow in your relationship with Jesus Christ. It offers time honoured clues that can help develop habits that put you in a position where Jesus can direct life. It puts forward basic practical things that will stand you in good stead as you are preparing for eternity. It gives you clues for helping others into the place where the spiritual reality of an ever-loving Jesus can become the dominant constant quality of any reconsecrated person you are helping" *Brethren, if anyone among you wanders from the truth, and someone turns him back, let him know that he who turns a sinner from the error of his way will save a soul from death and cover a multitude of sins.*[1]

Chapter 1

"THE WAY"[2] AHEAD

All Christians want to see people coming to Christ!

It is thrilling to be in a large crusade and see many people apparently receiving Jesus as their saviour at the end of the meeting. Unfortunately it is becoming evident that the era of successful large crusades, led by such people as D. L. Moody and more latterly Billy Graham and now his offspring, have lost their original impact. Not that big city-wide crusade's, in the western world, are not now being attempted with large numbers of people still responding. The culture has changed. Lately the greater number of contemporary responder's are people who are already church-goers. They are usually labelled: Reconsecrations!

With the passing of such evangelistically effective, big, multi-denominational crusades in the west, there was a reaction. Personal evangelism movements such as "Navigators," "Campus Crusade for Christ" etc sprang up, not only highlighting the evangelistic failings of such large crusades but stressing the lack of Biblical disciple making,. Further reaction came in the form of the Charismatic Movement underscoring the spiritual lack in the Church generally. In an effort to ascertain what was working evangelistically, the Church Growth Movement co-opted sociology and tried to sort out the wood from the trees.

Now, huge Youth Rallies are still occurring. Many young people are responding to an invitation to accept Christ but are not found in any church a month or so later. (The exception being if they were regular youth group attendees beforehand.) As earnestly dedicated as the proponents of such meetings are, it is being said in some cases "spiritual entertainment" is the only form of "discipleship" being employed. In spite of all this the corporate Church Body at large, no longer having big influxes of new believers, continues on with large crusades. These campaigns are now uncovering a pool of people, within the Churches, whose spirits are being stirred, often unknowingly gaining a yen to be discipled and fulfil the prompting of the Holy Spirit within them. Regularly these people are seen at the end of meetings, or at other times, privately reconsecrating themselves to Christ.

These reconsecrated people, because they are already church goers, most often fall back into whatever they were already doing or not doing before the event which brought them into notice. Actually, these people represent a group ready to learn how to be the resource the Church needs, to enliven it's self and build up the Body of Christ.

If we can only teach them how!

Too often in the past we have heard enthusiastic young believers being "counselled" by their older counterparts: *"Argh, you'll calm down and get over it soon!"* That's not teaching them anything except how to compromise their new life in Christ with their already existing worldly culture. The eagerness of a new believer is what the Church needs. The fervour of a fresh new life in Christ or the newly awakened love of an older believer should be fanned into the flame that will set the church on fire restoring the normality of Jesus desire to populate heaven with new disciples.

This book is not the latest high tech method of growing a Church rather it is designed to help hungry Christians into a fresh personal relationship with Jesus and thereby become healthier members of the Church Body, capable of making new disciples with that same attractive freshness they once found for themselves when they first came to Christ, giving motivation and purpose to the reconsecration they have just enacted.

If you have made a reconsecration recently at a public meeting, or in a regular Church meeting, or just quietly, personally, without anyone else's help, this book is for you. It is also for those who have witnessed this happening to friends and associates whom they feel constrained to now help progress in their Christian lives. In fact it would even be helpful to people coming to Christ for the first time.

ON "THE WAY"

Fuller Theological Seminary in the late 1980's, as part of their Church Growth courses, conducted a module called "Church Growth Pathology;" in it, one of the reasons given (#4) for lack of Church growth was "Hyper Co-operativism,"[3] this coming from the largest Interdenominational Seminary in the world? Fortunately they were quick to point out exceptions to the rule (EG, A Luis Palau crusade in Argentina resulting in many new Churches being planted and many added to existing Churches). It is also worth noting that co-operation within denominations fared no better than across denominations.

One of the problems was a dilution of the emphasis on the local Church. With local Churches beginning to assess their own cultures and develop their own Church vision and mission there has been a positive change. With people coming into Churches because of particular needs rather than because of special national or doctrinal positions there is a greater unity across denominations because of the common situations faced and the over-riding desire of Jesus for the unity of His Body.

Programmes such as "Transformations"[4] show how Churches can co-operate, across denominations, against the forces of evil, with amazing results not only for the Kingdom of God but for the health of the community at large.

One of the symptoms of the so-called Hyper-cooperative pathology was determined as "the follow up gap." In Biblical terms this meant there was no emphasis on making real disciples. So long as people came and sat in the church seats and stayed there every Sunday it was all OK. "Follow up" is not a Biblical term but "discipleship" is. This is still a problem in Churches now.

Often the teaching in Church follows the school class model - teacher + students. What is needed are principles that can be used to develop a person's own relationship with Jesus, learning to feed themselves daily on the word of God with prayer and fellowship, learning how to be led by the Spirit. For someone making a reconsecration these are the principles that should be espoused. To rely on Sunday to charge you up for the week following doesn't even work for the minister.

Campaigns of bringing people to Christ are changing with Churches co-operating to reach their communities for Christ but maintaining their own vision in the process. The success of these programmes is still dependent on each Church covering the discipleship gap. Campaigns such as "City Gospel Movements" with their "Movement Days" are leading the way in many countries. Local Churches are accepting responsibility for evangelising their own communities rather than relying on their distant denominational headquarters; getting together with other denominations. Now trusting each other, and Together reaching out to their own cities.

"The times, they are a changing." To look positively at what is happening now, one could say, there is a fresh wind of the Spirit beginning to blow across the Churches. Perhaps people reconsecrating are sensing it and looking to prepare themselves for whatever God wants to do. Could this be the last great move of the Spirit before Jesus comes again?

Chapter 2

EARLY ALONG "THE WAY"

Now that you have made a reconsecration (maybe more than one)! You are very sincere about it. What's going to stop everything going along as it always has and next week you'll need to make another reconsecration?

There has to be change!

If you go back into the same old rut you have been in that brought you to the place where you needed to make a reconsecration you will be in exactly the same place where you need to make another reconsecration again in no time.

There has to be change!

Do you really want to be used by God ... realise your potential ... bear much fruit? (more than you have in the past)

There has to be change!

Not a momentary change of opinion or a good thought about what you should do but a real change in lifestyle and priorities as a result of the operation of the Holy Spirit within. To squash the promptings of the Spirit[5] because you have to fit it all into your current life pattern will only result in frustration. God has to be allowed to order your life's pattern rather than have it pushed around by the pressures of your existence.

THE MOVING OF THE HOLY SPIRIT IN A
BELIEVER'S LIFE IS A WONDERFUL THING!

When God touches a life it is always for a great purpose[6]. It is always to change something that needs changing for the better[7].

What must be realised now is, if life goes along in the same manner it has always gone along then nothing new will happen. We must be prepared for radical changes in our day to day living if God is to be allowed to produce the changes He wants David Allen Hubbard, former President of Fuller Theological Seminary, observed: *Change carries risk. But so does resistance to change.*[8]

Same ole, same ole is the curse of vital spiritual life.

To keep on doing the same thing but expecting a different result is aggravated irritation.

New habits must be added to life to get rid of the aggravation and produce new life.

If you are willing to make God directed changes – read on!

INITIATING CHANGE

Obviously, you & God came to a conclusion that your relationship needs some adjustment, that's why you reconsecrated. Maybe you have been aware of this many times before. This time you are doing something about it.

If you are serious about this reconsecration there will be some unexpected outcomes

When you study the New Testament you will find there is a vast difference between what you see of the Church then and what you see now. As you read you may be impressed by the freshness of the Spirit of God that the early Christians had. You can have it too if you are prepared to spend time with God, as they did every day.

THE CHANGE MALADY

For many people change is like a drug – we must have it. Change for change sake is not healthy. It's the same as no change ever. Both are a state of being, influenced only by life's entertaining (or lack of it) expediency.

Having spent almost 10 years living in Asia it becomes obvious there are stark differences of cultural vista between west and east. Regardless of which one we adhere to, cultural norms can easily get in the way of seeing things the way Jesus wants us to see them – exactly what happened with the Pharisees. Jesus view of life was from an altogether different perspective. He saw things from a heavenly viewpoint and He continually tried to show us that. We are going to ultimately live in heaven so we need to learn how to see it from His point of view.

Jesus constantly taught in parables This parabolic view constantly tried to change earthly things into heavenly realities. *But we all, with unveiled face, beholding as in a mirror the glory of the Lord, are being transformed into the same image from glory to glory, just as by the Spirit of the Lord.*[9] [For more on parabolic visualization see Chapter 5; "Abiding means seeing things the Jesus way."]

Most changes are reactive – they come too late to maintain impetus, momentum and vision. Changes that see things Jesus way are proactive and make way for the development of a life realigning core values. Courage, foresight and purity of heart are the usual elements created first. Let that parabolic vision *"Keep your heart with all diligence, For out of it spring the issues of life."*[10]

Throughout the centuries the Church has consistently displayed the creativity of God. The Reformation of the 16th Century can be blamed for destroying much Church art but in diametric opposition it also came up with much creative theology. Who knows what creative ideas or issues the Holy Spirit may develop within you? There are several lists of gifts, both spiritual and natural, given in the scripture,[11] looking at these may be a starting point for whatever creative feature God wants to bring forth from you. Seeking out, allowing creative change to occur can be exciting, particularly when you see it having an impact on others around you.

Chapter 3

THE GOD WHO NEVER GIVES UP!

GOD LOVES YOU[12]

Yes, God loves the world OK, "*but He doesn't really love me!*" True for everyone else but not me. There seems to be so much sin and chaos in my world. What Jesus accomplished on the cross seems clouded and far away. How can he possibly love me after the way I have let him down.

Actually:

GOD LOVES YOU AND NEVER STOPS LOVING YOU

Nowhere in the scripture is Christ's finished work of forgiving all the sin of the world ever challenged. Regardless of who you are, what you have done or not done. No matter how much you have let Him down or failed to do things you know He wanted; what God wants to see, is, you, the object of his love, being fruitful and enjoying his Kingdom[13].

Having suffered great disillusionment and emotional pain, a young man who had once known God found himself confused, disoriented and away from his Father's house. "It seemed strange," he would later testify, "to find myself in a drunken state or a drug induced high, rejecting the God of my childhood and youth. A part of me still loved and wanted God and believed His ways were right, while another part of me seemed unable to find my way out of the fog."

"On several occasions, I remember the Holy Spirit's clear and quiet voice making itself heard over the clamour of loud music and marijuana-dulled senses. 'Why are you doing this?' (I knew the question was for me, not Him. He already knew very well my confusion.) 'You know this isn't who you really are. You belong to Me, and I won't let you go,' the Holy Spirit would gently remind me. It amazed me that He would pursue me in such places.

"At times I would leave the bar and walk for a while, high on drugs, yet communing with the God who wouldn't let me go. For a season I continued to blindly run the maze of my confused condition, crashing into pain after pain and disillusionment after disillusionment.

"Then one day, the not-to-be-denied love of God caught up with me and crashed through all my fears and facades. Another prodigal came to his senses, finding himself in the loving embrace of a heavenly Father whose determined love was greater than Satan's determined hatred and seemingly indestructible hold."

I know the young man of this story well. I can fill in all the gaps and read between all the lines. I understand his confusion, I can identify with his pain and I know the overwhelming power of the love and grace of God that he experienced. I know these things because I was that young man [14].

This is the testimony of Dutch Sheets, author of the great book "Intercessory Prayer [15]." In my opinion the best book recently written on prayer

How many "reconsecrations" did Dutch Sheets make before God really got hold of him and made him into an apostle and a world leader in the current prayer movement?

My own testimony is much the same. Coming to Christ at age eleven and experiencing the overwhelming power of God's love I spent the next 13 years wandering thru' wilderness after wilderness. Upon leaving school I spent the remainder of my teens and early twenties in an alcoholic haze. If I became drunk enough I would testify about Jesus or start an argument about creation instead of evolution. Even taking girls home they sometimes gained an impromptu sermon about Jesus despite former ignoble intentions. In spite of a reconsecration at my father's death during this period and other broken promises to do what I thought God wanted, I reached 24 years of age and married. Eight months later the Spirit of God took hold of me; another 18 months and I found myself in Bible College.

Even in the New Testament there were those who fell backwards but were reinstated to live fruit bearing lives. The infamous occasion when the Apostle Peter denied his Lord three times at Jesus' crucifixion [16] is the standout.

John Mark (cousin of Barnabus [17]), who began ministry with Paul and Barnabus [18], disgraced himself by not completing their ministry tour [19]. He became the object of division between Paul and Barnabus [20]. Paul would not take him on another missionary journey. It was left to Barnabus to restore him to ministry. This he did to Paul's satisfaction and once again the prodigal apostle became fruitful [21]. It is claimed, in many circles, that John Mark (converted thru' the Apostle Peter[22]) was the author of Mark's Gospel[23].

Demas was a respected member of Paul's ministry team [24]. He left the team, unnecessarily forsaking Paul. The reason given: he *"loved this present world[25]."* By the time Philemon was written he was forgiven and back in the apostolic fold[26].

All of these testimonies, both Biblical and contemporary, illustrate the loving nature of God, prepared to reconsecrate the wayward prodigal at any time.

The word consecrate is not really about a ceremony to open a building or some other formal event, it is best described in Hebrew as: *to be clean ... keep holy, purify, sanctify.* In New Testament Greek there are two words for consecrate, meaning *to complete, accomplish, consummate (in character); finish, fulfil, (make) perfect,* or, *to renew, dedicate[27].*

Whatever you have done, not done, left undone or otherwise transgressed the will of God. No matter how terrible or horrific, God still loves you and the blood of Jesus is still valid to cover your sin and lead you into a fruitful life.

The apostle Paul proves the point.

In Romans chapter 7 he laments his state. *For the good that I will to do, I do not do; but the evil I will not to do, that I practice.*[28]

In Romans chapter 8 his reconsecration is complete. *There is therefore now no condemnation to those who are in Christ Jesus, who do not walk according to the flesh, but according to the Spirit*[29].

God still loves you and wants to make your consecration or reconsecration alive and dynamic, filled with the fullness of His presence.

AND HE CAN DO IT!

Chapter 4

REVIEW

What really happened when you came to Christ originally?

Examine and test and evaluate your own selves to see whether you are holding to your faith and showing the proper fruits of it. Test and prove yourselves [not Christ]. Do you not yourselves realise and know [thoroughly by an ever-increasing experience] that Jesus Christ is in you--unless you are [counterfeits] disapproved on trial and rejected? But I hope you will recognise and know that we are not disapproved on trial and rejected.

2Corinthians 13:5, 6 Amp

GRACE

It was the grace of God that brought us to Christ not something deserved because we were good. Not something we earned because of what we did. Not something we worked out by our superior knowledge. It was a gift from God that we received. *For by grace you have been saved through faith, and that not of yourselves; it is the gift of God, not of works, lest anyone should boast.*[22]

REPENTANCE

Firstly, something happened to you that *"stung (cut to) the heart"*[30] because the Holy Spirit caused you to realise the grace of God had granted you repentance to life[31] thus inwardly knowing the truth[32] about Jesus. It was the goodness of God leading you to repentance.[33]

Old Testament prophet Zechariah anticipated this in chapter twelve, verse ten when the Holy Spirit said: *"And I will pour on the house of David and on the inhabitants of Jerusalem the Spirit of grace and supplication; then they will look on Me whom they pierced. Yes, they will mourn for Him as one mourns for his only son, and grieve for Him as one grieves for a firstborn."*

When someone behold's Jesus (*"me whom they pierced"*) they will (*"mourn ... and grieve"*) Ie.repent.

Repentance is not just a change of opinion – the worst of sinners know they have done the wrong thing. It is a realisation that God is involved and a consciousness of His holiness is taking place. There is an awesome awareness of the heavenly realm and a need to appropriate the salvation God is offering. The full impact of repentance now upon you! It is a realisation that God not only wants you to be aware of your previous sins that separated you from Him but now wants to deal with all the idiosyncrasies of your personality, repenting of all the small things that effect ungodly attitudes within you.[34] Developing the attitude of Jesus, becomes an on-going process.

Repentance is not just changing outlook. With the grace of God flowing thru' your spirit He measures you against the holiness of Jesus and prompts a response from your soul which will only be complete when it issues forth jointly from mind,[35] emotion[36] and will.[37] If it is reason alone it will only be opinion, if it is feelings alone it will be remorse, if it is will alone it is merely *"reshuffling the deck chairs on the Titanic."*

It is like a manual automobile in its garage. You, now in contact the Holy Spirit, want to take the car out. First you must start the engine - the emotional drive - the engine now roaring but the vehicle going nowhere; the emotions making a loud noise, giving off much unpleasant odour but the car still going nowhere. Next you need to select the gear – the mind deciding it wants to progress. Lastly you must engage the clutch – the will to actually go where the Spirit wants to go. All of these characteristics must work together, the engine running, gears engaged and clutch out to actually going where God intends.

Repentance is a wholehearted turning from something[38] and a turning to something.[39] A turning from all forms of sin and selfishness, turning to the loving embrace of Father God and our saviour The Lord Jesus Christ.

Comparing oneself to the Christians of the New Testament era makes one feel woefully inadequate? Perhaps it is because you have never before made a surrender as strong as the word repentance requires so that, with conversion, comes *"times of refreshing...from the presence of the Lord."*[40]

REDEMPTION

Next, you acknowledged the power of the cross of Christ to deal with your sin and you really turned away from that sin. Jesus said: *"I have not come to call the righteous, but sinners, to repentance."*[41]

You embraced the Gospel of Jesus.

Moreover, brethren, I declare to you the gospel which I preached to you, which also you received and in which you stand, by which also you are saved, if you hold fast that word which I preached to you—unless you believed in vain. For I delivered to you first of all that which I also received: that Christ died for our sins according to the Scriptures, and that He was buried, and that He rose again the third day according to the Scriptures, and that He was seen by Cephas, then by the twelve. After that He was seen by over five hundred brethren at once, of whom the greater part remain to the present, but some have fallen asleep. After that He was seen by James, then by all the apostles. Then last of all He was seen by me also, as by one born out of due time. For I am the least of the apostles, who am not worthy to be called an apostle, because I persecuted the church of God. But by the grace of God I am what I am, and His grace toward me was not in vain; but I laboured more abundantly than they all, yet not I, but the grace of God which was with me. Therefore, whether it was I or they, so we preach and so you believed.[42]

"Believing" was not just a matter of acknowledging the historical fact of the death, burial and resurrection of Jesus. The Preface to the

Amplified Version of the Bible says: *"Take as an example the Greek word* pisteuo, *which the vast majority of versions render "believe." That simple translation, however, hardly does justice to the many meanings contained in the Greek* pisteuo: *"to adhere to, cleave to, to trust, to have faith in; to rely on, to depend on." Consequently, the reader gains understanding through the use of amplification, as in John 11: 25: "Jesus said to her, I am [Myself] the Resurrection and the Life. Whoever believes in (adheres to, trusts in, and relies on) Me, although he may die, yet he shall live."*[43]

You can't decide on a compromise so that you don't appear too religious to your friends and acquaintances. It must be a belief in Jesus enabling you to treat others in the same manner as Jesus would treat them. It means seeking at all times to involve Jesus in everything you do, always seeking to have Jesus as Lord of all you think and do, seeking first the kingdom of God and His righteousness, so that all needed things are being added to your life.[44]

Salvation is about receiving Christ.[45]

FAITH...

...is the element that takes us into the heavenly realm. Faith is a two-way street. Me trusting Jesus to fulfil the promise of eternal life that he offers and him trusting me to live according to his commandments.[46]

Faith is not some sort of wish: "Yes, that's a nice story about Jesus, better than most, I like it, it'll be nice if it's true, I think I'll believe it - better than all the other options." This is not faith.

Faith is solid. It requires a whole of life response. *But without faith it is impossible to please Him, for he who comes to God must believe that He is, and that He is a rewarder of those who diligently seek Him.*[47]

Faith's confession – acknowledges openly and joyfully, celebrates and praises Jesus for his Calvary accomplishments, exalting and honouring our Lord as the one who brings power in applying faith to all of life right into eternity. It brings the reality of the Holy Spirit into obvious connection.

FELLOWSHIP

When Jesus comes into your life he wants to have a relationship with you.

A verse that has often been used to bring people to Christ was actually written to a church. In Revelation chapter 3 and verse 20 Jesus is standing outside the door of the church. [they must all have needed reconsecration – Rev 3: 16, 17] It doesn't say He is unknown to the church or the "community," as chapters 2 and 3 show. Rather he is consigned to a position where his presence is useless to either individual or group. He is knocking at the church door. Situations are occurring continually which are his knocking. This accident happens, that person dies prematurely, conflict occurs with this neighbour or that workmate, our immediate family needs are demanding, life hurries by and we are engrossed in its continued pressure – these are part of the myriad noises coming from Jesus knocking at our hearts door. Stopping our absorption with mundane existence and listening for his voice is paramount. He wants fellowship with us and he wants to challenge and enrich a fellowship with each other strengthening it as the book of Revelation embroils the Church (not just the individual) in the battle to victory at the end. True fellowship with Jesus and the Church must be constantly worked at to bring this triumph. The western individualistic view of salvation often denies the fact that it was the Church that brought them to Christ and it is the Church that is ultimately victorious. The best "lone ranger" Christians can do (if they do anything), is produce more selfish individuals doing their own thing[48] – a far cry from Jesus building his Church, no salvation in that.

FORGIVENESS

Jesus said to them again, "Peace be with you; as the Father has sent Me, I also send you." And when He had said this, He breathed on them and said to them, "Receive the Holy Spirit." If you forgive the sins of any, their sins have been forgiven them; if you retain the sins of any, they have been retained."[49]

We love to talk about the amazing things that happened on the Day of Pentecost and so we should. but, the most important thing that happened when the Holy Spirit was given, was the God-given ability to forgive.

So much of religion has to do with "superiority." 'I'm right (doesn't really matter what I believe) I'm right and your wrong.' In other words it's a prop that we believe in order to inflate our self esteem (or is it our self deception).

Who is right & who is wrong is not the issue – who is forgiving and who isn't is more to the point. (Not that we shouldn't be looking to believe right things) It's amazing to look & see what we should be right about – it's about living the way God says – forgiving others and removing them and us from bondage.

Then He [thoroughly] opened up their minds to understand the Scriptures, And said to them, Thus it is written that the Christ (the Messiah) should suffer and on the third day rise from (among) the dead, [Hos. 6:2.] And that repentance [with a view to and as the condition of] forgiveness of sins should be preached in His name to all nations, beginning from Jerusalem.]"[50]

Jesus' purpose was and still is to forgive sin and to use us to continue doing it!

"Judge not, and you shall not be judged. Condemn not, and you shall not be condemned. Forgive, and you will be forgiven.[51]

Failure to forgive is to condemn ourselves to bondage equal to the one we are failing to forgive. It puts us outside the will of God, censuring us to dry religious experience instead of fresh up-building relationship with Father, Son and Holy Spirit.

Jesus put forgiveness front and centre when the disciples asked Him to teach them how to pray. He said: *"And forgive us our sins, For we also forgive everyone who is indebted* [sinned against – Ed] *to us. And do not lead us into temptation, But deliver us from the evil one."*[52] This is a key to staying out of temptation and of deliverance from besetting evil.

BAPTISM

Regardless of the form expressing our introduction into the Christian Church it should translate into ...

"... the answer of a good conscience toward God, through the resurrection of Jesus Christ,"[53]

Chapter 5

LIVING IN THE KINGDOM

Abide in Me, and I in you. As the branch cannot bear fruit of itself, unless it abides in the vine, neither can you, unless you abide in Me.[54]

Abiding in Jesus is the key to living in the presence of God. When this happens assurance of salvation ceases to be theory, it becomes life. Faith is no longer just a good idea it is reality. There is positive resource and a destiny identifying with the goals of Jesus all the way into heaven.

Abiding in Christ is not just a theme of one chapter in the Bible,[55] it is everywhere. The Apostle John amplifies the theme of abiding in his first letter making twenty one direct references in the short five chapters.

The Apostle Paul doesn't use the word abiding but he continually refers to the same principle thru'out his manifold letters, using words such as: *"If we live in the Spirit, let us also walk in the Spirit."*[56] Or:*"I have been crucified with Christ; it is no longer I who live, but Christ lives in me; and the life which I now live in the flesh I live by faith in the Son of God, who loved me and gave Himself for me."*[57] Again: *"For to me, to live is Christ."*[58]

It's even in the Old Testament. Listen to Isaiah:*"But those who wait* [abide in – Ed] *on the LORD Shall renew their strength; They shall mount up with wings like eagles, They shall run and not be weary, They shall walk and not faint."*[59] Or even Moses: *"And He* (God) *said, "My Presence will go with you, and I will give you rest."*[60]

Mark Virkler sums it up: *"It is so easy to get caught up with the affairs of life that we totally lose our awareness that Christ is living within us. We find ourselves living on the surface of life and not discerning the spirit and heart at all. Many people are hardly aware that they even have a spirit, much less that Jesus speaks and gives life from within it."*[61]

THE SECRET OF A FRUITFUL LIFE

"I am the vine, you are the branches. He who abides in Me, and I in him, bears much fruit; for without Me you can do nothing.[62]

Jesus refers to himself as a vine. He refers to you and I as branches in that vine. We didn't start out as branches, we were made branches when we accepted Jesus and were lovingly grafted into his vine.

If you observe a grafting process you will note a bud (a place where new life is sprouting from the trunk of the tree) is taken out and the new branch grafted into its place. The new branch now has a position in the vine with the maximum advantage of excelling in growth, drawing on the life of the tree. The graft will always be in that place in the tree that is best for overall growth. For a short time it will be held in place by a special tape as it draws on the quintessence of the tree and finally becomes completely united with it while still maintaining its own branch integrity.

For existing unruly branches Jesus tells us there are two alternatives: pruning[63] or removal.[64]

Pruning may hurt for a while but the removal of unfruitful branches is best for the ultimate growth of the branch and the vine. Pruning becomes more than bearable when we realise we are a positive part of the greater infinite plan of Jesus (the vine) building his church on into eternity.

Jesus said: *"I will build my church,"* abiding in Christ enables him to do it thru' us.

THE "LIBERATION" OF ABIDING

Jesus died to take the heat out of every drop of bitterness, hurt, rejection or rebellion that comes our way. Abiding in him releases us from these negativities. Hanging on to them, feeling sorry for ourselves, developing antagonisms, self justification, wrong attitudes, etc can all be reversed when we learn to abide in him. Hanging on to them separates us from Jesus. proving the scripture in Proverbs 18: 1 *"A man who isolates himself seeks his own desire; he rages against all wise judgement."* Jesus wants to release his love and forgiveness thru' us, give us the inward peace that does away with all the habitual mind-sets that continually occupy our attention and block the Spirit of God tendering the peace of God to our spirit and soul giving us the inner platform to produce the positive fruit of the spirit.

ABIDING MEANS RELEASE

Think, for a moment, about your up-bringing. Your parents, siblings, school friends, teachers and community associates all contributed to your opinion of yourself. Ground zero (you) learned how to deal with set-backs, problems etc usually reinforced by the attitudes of your acquaintances. Often you would react with fear, shame, depression, anger or some other self- condemnatory attitude. When something went wrong you could go around in circles in that self -contemptible mind-set. Depression, rage or withdrawal could set in at your lack of ability to deal with the outcome of whatever had happened. Abiding in Jesus may not be the quick-fix that you are looking for but it is the only way of a perpetual, consistent attitude that will not only deliver you from the unpleasant result of what has just happened but will keep you in a place, not governed by the events of the past, no matter who has contributed to them. It will keep you in the comfort of your relationship with God and ultimately make a positive way forward.

What God thinks about you is more important than what anyone else (including you) thinks about you. God loves you – live in it! *"As the Father loved Me, I also have loved you; abide in My love."* said Jesus.[65] Don't say: 'God loves everybody else but he couldn't possibly love me after all I have gone thru' and the things I have done. To say that denies all that Jesus went thru' on Calvary – he expressly did it for the things you did. Turn away from them and enjoy the freedom of God's love. Confessing sin to him,[66] consistently receiving his forgiveness and returning to the abiding relationship.

ABIDING MEANS REST

In amongst all the hurley-burley of competitive living within today's society there are more people opting out by suicide than ever before. There are now myriad organizations desperately attempting to staunch this loss of valuable life-source. Sometimes these individuals are capable of great positive impact on the lives around them, instead (Eg Robin Williams), opting out of a troubled existence into a troubled eternity.

Jesus had the answer to this – learn how to abide in him.

Moses, the governor of three million rebellious people on a 40 year wilderness hike learned it: *"My Presence will go with you, and I will give you rest"*[67] God said it to him and meant it.

Now *"a promise remains of entering His rest"*[68] for us - abide in Christ! Knowing about this is not enough, believing in it is not enough. We must enter into it, constantly doing so in our daily routine. Eternal life doesn't start when we die, it begins the moment we receive Christ. Hebrews chapter 4 is using the disobedient Children of Israel as a physical example of a spiritual principle, not entering into the promise of God, dying in the wilderness instead. Only two individuals, Joshua and Caleb, who left Egypt, arrived in the promised land. The remainder were a new generation.

ABIDING MEANS REFOCUSING

People generally are much happier living within accustomed limits, to stray outside these brings an uncertainty, disrupting comfort. There is no fresh progress staying there. Abiding in Christ plucks us out of that self induced comfort zone and puts us in the position of trusting someone else for life outcomes – Jesus. The testimony of Jesus earthly-life reveals he by no means lived his life or went thru' his excruciating death for his own ends. It was to reconcile God's creation back to Him. Abiding in Christ puts us in the position of being his agent in that process. It removes us from our self-induced coma into a positive fresh way of life.

For I know the thoughts that I think toward you, says the LORD, thoughts of peace and not of evil, to give you a future and a hope.[69]

Learning to Abide in Christ captures God's thoughts for you. To help this happen we need to learn how to meditate on the scripture.

Joshua was right on the money when he said: *This Book of the Law shall not depart from your mouth, but you shall meditate in it day and night, that you may observe to do according to all that is written in it. For then you will make your way prosperous, and then you will have good success.*[70] Asking God to give you scriptures for your own life and for your family and then analysing them and working out what you should do about them is a sure way to success.

Living in constant touch with the Holy Spirit and relating to him at all times is the way forward in abiding in Christ. Not making big noises to all in sundry around you but quietly being what God wants in any situation. God will eventually supply others who will want what you have.

Then Jesus said to those Jews who believed Him, *"If you abide in My word, you are My disciples indeed. And you shall know the truth, and the truth shall make you free."*[71]

ABIDING MEANS SEEING THINGS THE JESUS WAY

"Is the glass half full or is the glass half empty?"

Obviously the answer to this question depends upon how you look at it. Fortunately there are more ways of looking at things than the optimistic/pessimistic paradigm. For example, we could try the parabolic reference frame. This is the one that Jesus used.

We know that Jesus constantly taught in parables *"All these things Jesus spoke to the crowds in parables, and He did not speak to them without a parable"*[72] except when He used a metaphor.

Since Jesus constantly taught in parables He must have constantly thought in parables. Since He constantly thought in parables He must have consistently lived in parables. It could even be said that His life was a parable!

What is a parable? In Sunday School we learned that a parable was 'an earthly story with a heavenly meaning.'

When Jesus looked at something He didn't see optimism/pessimism He saw heavenly reality. What He saw had eternal ramifications. He was abiding in the Father and the Father was abiding in Him. So everything He saw, everything He touched, everything He did was a picture of heaven. Many people saw but didn't see, heard but didn't hear.[73] Jesus spent a lot of time teaching His disciples to see parabolically, it's something we need to master also.

To see life situations in a parabolic or metaphorical manner can transform an otherwise ordinary situation into something that can shape our lives and direct our destinies. It can cause us to "climb the ladder of success" rather than "struggle to keep our head above water." It's the difference between being an ugly earthbound caterpillar or a beautiful soaring butterfly.

The parabolic vision is much more than earthly optimism it is knowing the Divine empowering available, seeing the eternal potential ahead and living in the abiding parable of a holy life.

[For further teaching on the topic of Abiding: see "Walking on the Inside," © Dr Colin Crago 2015, published by Tate Publishing & Enterprises LLC, Mustang Oklahoma.]

Chapter 6

EMBRIONIC RELATIONSHIP

When you fell in love (or if you would like to fall in love) you want to spend time with the object of that love. That person becomes someone you want to be with so you go out of your way to make time and place where you can facilitate the relationship. If you are going to avail yourself of the love Jesus is offering the same thing must take place. You will need to make time and a place to develop that relationship. This will have to be a priority or the relationship will divorce (the very reason why so many marriages fail).

There is a quaint story about a young man and a young woman who went out on a date one night. Following the evening's entertainment they were sitting, talking together in his automobile, outside the young lady's home. In the process of the lengthy discussion the topic turned to literature, he asked her if she had read a particular book. She replied "yes." "What did you think of it he asked?" "Not much," she replied." "I wrote that book," was his awkward reply. The meeting broke up; she went into her house, found the book, began reading it again and when she had finished decided it was the best book she had ever read. What caused the change of opinion? Answer she now had a relationship with the author. If you want to get the most from reading the Bible you need to develop your relationship with the author – the blessed Holy Spirit who reveals both Father and Son.

ILLUMINATION

When you go to the optometrist to check your eyesight he will tell you, as he decides if you need glasses or not, light is the thing you need more than anything else for the health of your eyes. In your efforts to develop spiritual insight the same could be said – you need spiritual illumination. This doesn't come from the sun it comes from the Son, by means of Holy Spirit optics.

This comes about by two individual means – prayer and Word of God. Plus two correlations – other people, inside and outside the church. Let's consider the first two – the others depend very much on how you develop your individual responses.

BEGINNING DAILY RENEWAL

Today is a day of increased productivity, increased efficiency, increased pressure and increased stress and strain. There are more personal burnouts, marriage breakdowns and suicides than ever before. Society has lost its heritage and is paying the price.

Society's hustle and bustle decrees that unless something is done it will consume the patrons of its advancement.

Long ago the prophet Isaiah found the secret of rising above the hurley-burley and exploitation of his time. In chapter 40 verses 28 to 31 of his prophecy he says:*"Have you not known? Have you not seen? The everlasting God, the Lord, the Creator of the ends of the earth, neither faints nor is weary. His understanding is unsearchable. He gives power to the weak, and to those who have no might He increases strength. Even the youths shall faint and be weary, and the young men shall utterly fall. **But those who wait on the Lord** shall renew their strength: they shall mount up with wings like eagles, they shall run and not be weary, they shall walk and not faint"*

Things were bad in Isaiah's day too; youths were fainting and young men falling. However, the prophet tapped into an eternal answer. *"Waiting on the Lord"* is a secret that men and women of God, throughout history, have found is essential to living a life that overcomes both the mundane and the overwhelming. In fact, as Robert Foster points out:

"Everyman whoever became somebody for God had this
at the core of his priorities ... Time alone with God?"[74]

THE SECRET OF GREAT MEN AND WOMEN OF GOD

The bible is full of illustrations of men and women who discovered the wonderful secret of time spent alone with God in daily heart renewal. Abraham,[75] Moses,[76] Daniel,[77] Jesus himself,[78] and His Apostles[79] to name a few.

The brilliant scientist, Sir Issac Newton, said that he could take his telescope and look millions and millions of miles into space. Then he added: *But when I lay it aside, go into my room, shut the door, and get down on my knees in earnest prayer, I see more of heaven and feel closer to the Lord than if I were assisted by all the telescopes on earth."* We are all naturally weak and need strength, fearful and need courage, ignorant and need wisdom, wayward and need guidance, sinful and need restoration. Waiting on God in the *"Daily Renewal Time"* is where this strength, courage, wisdom, guidance and restoration is supplied.

The strength of any relationship is determined by the amount of time the participants spend together and how well they know and understand each other's needs. God understands what we need better than we do. We not only need to know what he knows about us but we need to know him personally and what he wants for he is God not us!

ESTABLISH PRIORITIES

But seek first the kingdom of God and His righteousness,
and all these things shall be added to you.[80]

Putting God first and spending time alone with him first thing in the day will enable God's Holy Spirit to go to work in our lives and reveal God's loving heart toward us and his purpose for us.

The Psalm writer of old had discovered the secret:

My voice You shall hear in the morning, O LORD; In the
morning I will direct it to You, And I will look up.[81]

The morning is by far the best time to wait on the Lord. But if you are a mother with young children or a shift worker or otherwise significantly time-challenged then work out the best time you can give regularly and expect to develop your relationship with Jesus thru' it.

Alfred Gibbs sums it up well: *"No one can begin the day well, go on well, or end up well who fails to make provision for this 'Quiet Time' with God. This period must be deliberately reserved and consciously kept for God. Nothing should be allowed to interfere with it for nothing can compensate the Christian for its loss. The devil, the world and the flesh will combine in their attempts to crowd it out of the day's programme, on the pleas that 'there is no time;' but time must be made and maintained for it if one's character and testimony are to count for Christ."*[82]

As a necessity to business success, all business leaders advocate making time amidst the furore of commerce for daily inventory and planning. Many busy men have also found that there is no substitute for making time for God to daily order the priorities of their lives. Far more can be accomplished in a day when the busyness is locked out for an unhurried renewal time allowing God to order and empower their day.

Martin Luther, the great Reformation leader of the 16th century was once reputed to have said: *I have so much to do tomorrow that I will need at least three hours of prayer in the morning to get it all done.*

Luther, like others, found that the more he had to do the more power he needed from God and the more prayer he needed to ensure its achievement.

The Catholic, Ignatius Loyola, founder of the Jesuit Order, was another who taught the necessity of a great daily disciplined time with Jesus.

PLAN YOUR PRAYER AND PRAY YOUR PLAN

What we all need is a workable plan for both getting started and keeping going in this vital matter of daily renewal. It's not much use trying to emulate Martin Luther or Ignatius Loyola and finding we have not got the motivation, resource or experience to spend such amounts of time profitably. **It's also much better to spend a consistent, regular time every day** than be up and down not knowing whether today will be a day with God or not or how much time we are going to spend and what we are going to do in it.

Seven minutes has often been advocated as a workable time for someone to begin daily renewal times who has never kept them before. However, bear in mind, this is a start of an adventure with God, so be prepared to increase the time as the days go by and experience grows.

FIRST: *wake up and get up!*

It's no good trying to renew your bed. To renew and revive your spirit you must be alert; bed is no place to do that. Shower and do whatever else is necessary to ensure you have maximum physical vigilance. Going to bed at an appropriate time the night before is another way to ensures sprightly attitude.

NEXT: ensure your spiritual attitude is alert.

THEN – T.A.P. into R.E.S.T.

T.A.P. means begin with **T**hanksgiving **A**nd **P**raise

Psalm 100 verse 4 is a good pattern.

Enter into His gates with thanksgiving, And into His courts with praise. Be thankful to Him, and bless His name.

Begin by giving thanks to God for the things he has done for you; for your salvation; for his Holy Spirit in your life; for the fellowship of the Church you share in; for the material blessings you share in (no matter how poor they may seem, what you have is worth having and will be better than what millions of others have); ask the Holy Spirit to prompt you about other items and then move into praise. Don't be scared to make some noise about this. Sing if you feel so constrained.

Praise God for who he is and for what he has done, particularly for what he achieved in sending Jesus to the cross.

If you are baptised in the Holy Spirit, expect the Spirit of God to cause you to speak in other tongues. If you are not, ask God to baptise you in His Spirit and look forward to the time when this will happen in the near future (perhaps even now – straight away!) Ask your pastor about it at your next opportunity. Speak in tongues as often as possible, you will find God can use this as another means to enliven your spirit and your prayer life.

R.E.S.T. is a good format for the remainder of your time. To rest and abide in Him is the goal of the relationship which God has spoken of in John chapter 15 and Hebrews chapter 4.

Following T.A.P. God will likely move you to **R**epent of any unconfessed sin in your life. If things are not going so well this may need to be addressed much sooner.

Expect the Holy Spirit to move in your life and produce faith in your heart.

Begin to **S**upplicate (pray earnestly with vigour and enthusiasm) for the desires of God and the needs of others. Follow this with your own personal petitions. Conclude your prayers, as you began, with **T**hanksgiving for the way God is answering your prayer.

It is a good habit to spend as much time in studying the scripture (encouraging God to talk to you) as you do in prayer (talking to him). If you have an assigned bible study, now would be good time to do it. If not, (or if the study is not enough) begin to read one of the Gospels (the book of John is a good one to start with). Read half a chapter or perhaps a whole chapter. Especially ask God to show you something of himself or something he specifically wants you to know – conclude by praying about this.

Remember: this is a guide not a law! Because you are exposing yourself to the love of God, very soon you will find 7 minutes has become 15 and it will not be long before you are absolutely engrossed in what God is doing and 30 minutes have passed like a flash.

WATCH OUT...!

Make sure you avoid the trap of worshipping the Renewal Time itself – Jesus is the one who should receive your accolades. If guilt comes because you miss out on a time one day, just remember that God is not dependent upon your performance to do what ever he wants to do. Confess your failure and make yourself available to God to use you anyway. Thank God that he still loves you just as much as he always has and is still able to use you in whatever situation you are confronted with. The world is tired of phony's. The only way we will ever make any impression on such a cynical population is by the genuineness of true faith. D.L.Moody, the famous evangelist of yesteryear is reputed to have said: *"character is what a man is in the dark."* We are what we really are when no one else can see us. What we really are should be what God intended we should be, not covering up what we really are with a lot of religious words and pseudo deeds. **A daily renewal time is the place where God can change our inside so we can become more like him.**

CONCLUSION

If such a renewal time was necessary for the Lord Jesus, then it is obviously necessary for us also. Mark 1: 35 says of Jesus:

Now in the morning, having risen a long while before daylight, He went out and departed to a solitary place; and there He prayed.

The Lord Jesus knew how to rise up above the dilemma and the people problems that assaulted him, soaring over the besetting problems like the eagle Isaiah wrote about.

Tomorrow morning is the time to start your renewal time. Will you covenant with Jesus to meet with him then?

Chapter 7

EMPOWERING RELATIONSHIP

Christianity is growing faster now than at any other time since its fledgling days. In the vanguard of this amazing growth are the churches of the "third" world. Churches in Latin America, Africa and Asia have far surpassed in size their older European counterparts.

The largest churches of most denominations in the world are now found in Korea not in England, Germany or even the United States of America.

What makes these churches grow in such a vital way?

There is a one word answer to this question and it's this:

PRAYER.

Many of these nations have been in a place of immanent distress and/or conflict for many years. They have reacted in much the same way as King David did when faced with the same problem.

> *"In my distress I called upon the Lord,*
> *Yes, I cried to my God;*
> *And from His temple He heard my voice,*
> *And my cry for help came into His ears.*
> *...He delivered me..."*[83]

Western nations are beginning to get a glimpse of troubles coming in the future for them also. Unfortunately many Christians have not read the signs of the approaching end and they are not prepared for the anarchy and fear that is not far ahead. Unless they learn the secret that King David learned their "faith" will be worthless.

THE ANSWER.

Another David (David Wilkerson) draws attention to the much needed solution: *"Repeatedly believers in our congregation and in others have heard their shepherds beg them to set aside a time each day to meet the Lord in secret prayer! Only those who learn to pour out their hearts to the Lord in the secret closet of prayer will be rewarded with a holy faith and trust!*

You see, communion gives birth to trust. Only by pouring out to God all our fears and worries can we come away with His rest and assurance. 'Trust in Him at all times...pour out your heart before Him'[84]. *Trusting and pouring out are inseparable!"*[85]

King David had learned the secret of spending time with his God in daily renewal. It wasn't just a time every day to fulfill some religious obligation. He learned to relate to God in such a way that in the face of overwhelming odds he had unshakeable confidence the relationship would deliver him, and it did.

And he said: "The LORD is my rock and my fortress and my deliverer; The God of my strength, in whom I will trust; My shield and the horn of my salvation, My stronghold and my refuge; My Saviour, You save me from violence. I will call upon the LORD, who is worthy to be praised; So shall I be saved from my enemies.[86]

Again, heed the words of David Wilkerson: ***"There are believers today who regularly shut themselves in with God and are getting to know Him - and that intimacy is giving birth to great trust!*** *Sitting under strong preaching, listening to tapes, worshiping and praising in the house of the Lord - all these activities are commendable and profitable. But none provides the strength you need to stand firm in times of trouble! Nothing will build you up in trust and confidence as much as secret, daily prayer with your heavenly Father!*

*You must have a place where you can go to meet with God every day!
You can't have a problem you won't give to Him, a burden you won't place
upon Him. And you can't leave His presence until you come away assured,
leaning upon His everlasting arms!"*[87]

Yet another David, Dr. David Yonggi Cho, former pastor of the
worlds largest church (of over 750,000 adult members), has repeatedly
insisted that all Christians should spend at least an hour a day in prayer
(and ministers should spend 3 hours).

Dr Dick Eastman has produced a book entitled *"The Hour That
Changes The World"*[88] advocating the same principle and giving a plan
for how to do it.

GODLY PRIORITY.

Giving God the first/best part of the day is the secret of any Spirit-
filled life. Without it spiritual poverty soon comes about. Psa 90:14
(NIV) says: *"Satisfy us in the morning with your unfailing love, that we
may sing for joy and be glad all our days."*

For some people, shift workers and the like, the day does not begin
in the morning and the best part of the day may not be the A. M. But for
the majority, even those affirmed "night owls" among us, the morning
is by far the best time to get with God and plan our day.

The importance of this daily renewal time cannot be underestimated.
It is here that we undertake development of the most important
relationship of our lives - our relationship with almighty God. It is here
we learn what the will of God is for us. It is here that God empowers
us to carry out what He wants.

It is reputed that the great Scottish reformer John Knox once had
his daily time with God disturbed by the incessant knocking on the
door by a friend. When he finally opened the door the friend informed
him that the King of England had come to visit him. Knox reputedly
replied: "You tell the King of England that I am meeting with the King
of the Universe, and I won't be interrupted by him."

The effective daily early morning renewal time really begins the
night before. We can't expect to spend quality time with God in the
morning if we are so tired we can't concentrate adequately when we
wake up. Perhaps this is what Isaiah is talking about when it says: *My*

soul yearns for you in the night; in the morning my spirit longs for you.[89] If my attitude (my soul) is right toward Him the night before, my spirit will be hungry enough to spend class time with Jesus the following morning.

"Drifting off" is a classic problem of renewal times. Instead of getting alone with God we have drifted off into some private reverie which only frustrates us later because we realize we have wasted time and missed the goal of spending time with the one we love. To help avoid this, Psalm 100 is a good pattern.

A MODEL.

Shout for joy to the LORD, all the earth. Worship the LORD with gladness; come before him with joyful songs. Know that the LORD is God. It is he who made us, and we are his; we are his people, the sheep of his pasture. Enter his gates with thanksgiving and his courts with praise; give thanks to him and praise his name. For the LORD is good and his love endures forever; his faithfulness continues through all generations.[90]

Singing is a great way to begin a Renewal Time (Verses 1 & 2). The Psalmist says: *Awake, my soul! Awake, harp and lyre! I will awaken the dawn."*[91] and again; *"I will sing aloud of thy mercy in the morning."*[92]

If singing doesn't usher you into the manifest presence of God try shouting as verse one suggests. Perhaps, because of your location and the risk of disturbing others you can't shout very loud then 'shout and sing on the inside.' At least enter into the joy that the Holy Spirit says (Verse 1) should characterize your "shouting" and "singing."

Appreciating who God really is (verse 3) always tends to alert us to God's presence. No one can sincerely contemplate who God is without having their mind awakened. Consider that God inhabits the ends of the universe and try to expand your mind to take Him in. Next, contemplate the fact that God inhabits the smallest atom adjacent to you.

The so called "Lord's Prayer" (actually Jesus made many prayers so this one would be better termed "a model prayer") begins with an injunction to contemplate the holy nature of God (*"hallowed be Thy name"*). Verse 5 suggests the same thing: *"For the LORD is good and his love endures forever; his faithfulness continues through all generations."*

A true understanding of God's goodness and mercy is an essential basis for any Christian life. If the Christian does not have this they will forever be caught in spiritual insecurity for themselves or legal judgment of others. Comprehending God's faithfulness is a lifetime reflection that will always yield spiritual confidence and maturity. A concordance is a useful tool to use in the pursuit of further understanding of God's goodness, love and faithfulness.

Of course any emphasis upon the true nature of God, particularly through the pages of Scripture, should lead to **a significant time of thanksgiving** (verse 4). All of the great feasts of the Old Testament (Passover, Pentecost & Tabernacles) were designed specifically as symbols of thankfulness for things God had done for the nation of Israel. In the New Testament the exhortation is to *"in everything give thanks"*[93] [*"in everything"* NOT *'for everything'*].

No matter what hardship you may be going through there is always something you can thank God for; if it's not immediately apparent go back to the last thing you can think of that you can thank God for and start there. If your mind has really been "hallowing" God it will not be long before your thanksgiving will remove any depression that may be there.

There are a great many things about your own person that you should be able to thank God for, no matter how you may feel you have missed out on the 'beauty' or 'brains' or something else that is currently in vogue. Everyone needs to thank God that they are uniquely made to fit into a matchless role in the Kingdom of God that no other being can fit into. God loves you exactly the way you are and its high time you began to thank Him for all those peerless assets that only you posses.

It should not be long before thanking Him for what He has done gives way to **praising His name** (verse 5). Thanksgiving has to do with thanking God for what He has done, praising Him has to do with thanking Him for who He is - for His very own self.

If you started with singing there's no reason why you can't do it again now. The Christian heritage is full of rich praise songs that can help you tell God how wonderful He is. The psalms, old hymns and modern songs all have something to offer. Colossians 3:16 says: *"Let the word of Christ dwell in you richly ... as you sing psalms, hymns and spiritual songs with gratitude in your hearts to God."* It could well be that the creative energy of the Holy Spirit will begin to flow through you and before long you are creating brand new praises to your God with soul stirring freshness. Even if you can't keep in tune God is still able to flow through you and bring forth His creative worship abilities.

Speaking in Tongues is a vehicle for the moving of the Holy Spirit and the stirring of the prayer life. To allow God's Spirit to flow through you while you focus upon the object of your prayer is to draw on resources beyond yourself and overcome blockages that otherwise might occur. If it is really allowing the Holy Spirit to flow, not just rehearsing what you have heard before in your mind and emotions, It can charge the 'spiritual batteries.'

"THE WORD."

Meditating upon the scripture (see Chapter 8, Enlisting The Word) is an essential part of any time spent with the Master. Psalm 1 is a great example.*Blessed is the man who does not walk in the counsel of the wicked or stand in the way of sinners or sit in the seat of mockers. But his delight is in the law of the LORD, and on his law he meditates day and night. He is like a tree planted by streams of water, which yields its fruit in season and whose leaf does not wither. Whatever he does prospers.*[94] (Verses 1-3)

It is best to read scripture systematically. The Holy Spirit can quicken a word to you no matter where you are reading. Hudson Taylor, the great missionary statesman of yesteryear, speaks of a situation where he was confronted by a state of particular spiritual adversity and personal spiritual dryness. His appointed scripture reading for that morning was a particularly repetitious passage from numbers 6 & 7. He felt to read something else that would be more uplifting but eventually returned to the set reading with a perfunctory prayer for the Lord to bless him. He says: *"oh! how abundantly it was answered and what a feast God gave me!* From this came the book 'Separation and Service.'*[95]

A balanced understanding of the scripture is much better than flitting from here to there. As Hudson Taylor found out, God can bless you from any part of His Word if your attitude is right. If things are dry it's your attitude that needs changing not your allocated portion of scripture.

There are many Bible reading schemes that will help you read systematically through the pages of the scripture. Your pastor will recommend one that will suit you. Get into it and stick to it.

When you read the scripture ask it questions - what, why, when, how, etc. The answer to these questions will enliven your reading and provide practical outworking for your life.

This technique was once used as the subject for a poem by Rudyard Kipling. It goes like this:

> *"I keep six honest serving men*
> *(They taught me all I knew);*
> *Their names were Where and What and When*
> *And Why and How and Who."* [96]

Perhaps you can use the verse analysis method of studying the scripture. Look for God to quicken a verse (verses, passage, half a verse etc.) to you. When you have made the selection write down answers to the following questions.

1. What is the thought preceding the verse

    (Summarize in a few words the context of the previous paragraph)?

2. What is the thought following the verse

    (summarize in a few words the context of the following paragraph}?

3. Write out the verse in your own words -

    PARAPHRASE IT! (Keep the paraphrase as accurate as possible).

4. Is there a command, a promise, a warning, an example to follow or an error to avoid?

5. What does this passage teach about God the Father, Jesus the Son or the Holy Spirit?

6. Can you find any cross-references from any other part of the bible to this passage?

(The centre or side margins of your Bible may help)

7. What do you intend to do with what you have found out?

David sums it up when he says: *"Oh, how I love your law! I meditate on it all day long. I have more understanding ..., for I obey your precepts' Long ago I learned from your statutes that you established them to last forever."*[97]

CONCLUSION.

Time alone with God in daily renewal is the secret of spiritual life. There really is no other way. The prophet Jeremiah was in more trouble than most of us yet in the depth of his lamentation he knew: **"Because of the Lord's great love we are not consumed, for his compassions never fail. They are new every morning; great is your faithfulness."**[98]

Jesus waits every morning to meet with you. It's something He does because of His great regard for you. Covenant with Him now that you will be there every morning to meet with Him.

Chapter 8

EMBELLISHING RELATIONSHIP

All people from the beginning of time have spent much of it praying. From early idolatry to developed systems; to modern psychological manipulations; even in war ("aint no atheists in the fox holes!") this has been the case.

What differentiates Christian prayer from all of the prayers offered by all of the idolatry, psychological twists and magical incantations in existence?

Short answer: Christian prayer starts with God and ends with what God does!

All of the encouragement to spend long periods in prayer is to get this to happen; to join the human spirit with the Divine, in an attempt to fulfil the plans of the Almighty for the best functioning of His universe.

Most "prayers" have to do with what the proponent happens to want, whatever he/she considers best for their immediate situation and comfort. Little thought is given to what others may want for their personal situations. It is easy to see there could be millions of "prayers" being offered in all manner of conflicting directions. Enough to give God nightmares if He didn't already have a plan for where things should go, His problem is to stop us sinning and to line up with what He wants.

REAL PRAYER

The late Professor O. Hallesby described prayer as *"Breath of the Soul;"* Naturally, if we don't breathe we die.[99]

Cameron V. Thompson defines prayer as *"the spreading out of our helplessness and that of others in the name of the Lord Jesus Christ before the loving eyes of a Father who knows and understands and cares and answers. Prayer is the breathing and panting of the spirit after God. It is taking hold of the willingness of God, rather than an overcoming of His reluctance. It is a tuning in on the great, thunderous, two- thousand-year- old prayer meeting going on in the glory above."*[100]

Here is what God said to King Solomon: *"Blessed is the man who listens to me, Watching daily at my gates, Waiting at the posts of my doors. For whoever finds me finds life, And obtains favour from the LORD";*[101]

Someone else has correctly said: *"The Gospel moves at a slow and timid pace when the saints are not at their prayers early and late and long."*

Prayer is not some sort heavenly shopping list presented to the Divine complete with empty shopping trolley just waiting to be filled. It is a hungering after God with such devotion that we find out what he wants and our communication with him is all toward fulfilling what He wants both in our own lives and in every part of God's creation that we touch.

George and Meg Patterson correctly say: *"prayer is not like ordinary language, for its true impetus is not what I have to say to God but what God has to say to me. Then, being apprehended and accepted by me, is returned to God as being His will for empowerment. This need not be in any clearly articulated manner, but as Paul said, 'with groanings which cannot be uttered'*[102].*"*[103]

If we can be in the flow of God's Spirit constantly, it will be amazing how we see answers to prayer come forth. Prayer is something we should be doing consistently, both personally and with others.

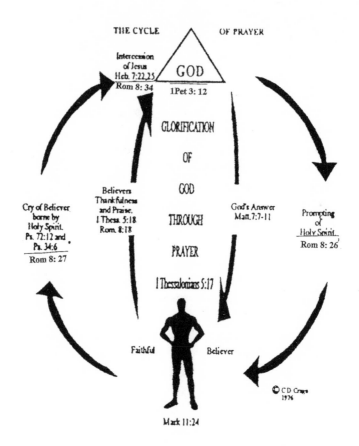

Prayer is a cycle – the Holy Spirit prompts us to cry out according to the will of God, Jesus interprets our prayer at the throne of Grace, God answers and we praise and thank Him then it starts again.

JESUS TAUGHT US HOW TO PRAY

In contravention to modern theological colleges the disciples never asked Jesus to teach them how to preach, they, knowing where the power came from, asked Him to teach them how to pray.[104]

The first principle He taught them was to acknowledge the altogether difference of the heavenly God culture – holiness. The alarming feature is the ability we think we have to change and add to this. Jesus, in telling us how to approach our *Heavenly Father,* started out with: *"Hallowed be Your name."* In other words be cognisant that whatever we consciously do in appreciating and asserting the person of our Father, value adds to the perceived holy reality of His person. Holiness is not just staying away from naughty things; groups that major on this often become so absorbed with what they are against, it eventually overtakes them. It has been labelled a Church Growth negative.[105] Holiness is about ascribing greatness to our wonderfully creative, gracious, compassionate, loving Heavenly Father and allowing our mind, emotions and will to be enlarged in the process as His nature is developed in us.

When this happens our desire is for His *"kingdom to come."* Unfortunately our kingdom seems to take precedence as we fail to practically understand He is more interested in "our kingdom" than we are.[106] If we put Him first we can draw on His power to straighten us up and expand the influence of our realm.

Here is where the clash usually occurs: *"Your will be done."* How many times have you advertently or inadvertently instructed God in how He should run His business? 'Help God I need you to do this or that!' Looking for the easiest path thru' a particular problem when all the time God is saying you need to go thru' it to develop a new prototype for future similar circumstances you are yet unaware will arise. It is so easy to forget God is running an eternal universe and our small yet important part in it must be subservient to the whole. When we fully apprehend it in our spirits, heaven can come down to earth.

Getting *our daily bread* is no longer much of a problem for the western world, so much so we take it for granted, often forgetting to thank God. In the third world it is still a major dilemma.

The foremost problem for us all is the "F" word – *forgiveness!* Nothing much happens without it. Lack of real forgiveness dulls our spirit, makes us, at best, powerlessly religious. Jesus is very plain about it – if I am expecting God's forgiveness for my sin I had better get started forgiving those who have done me wrong. Jesus re-emphasises it in the following verses of Matthew 6: 14 – 15 and 18: 21 - 35

Not blaming God for *"leading us into temptation"* is essential. He is actually wanting to *"deliver us from"* every demonic influence. This puts us back where we started: hallowing God and acknowledging all power and glory are His in His kingdom.

The Spirit of God knows our weakness and our ignorance. According to Romans 8: 26, He communicates with us deeply, in ways we don't understand, stirring our spirits, even causing us to groan in our spirits as He works His will within us.

Practising what we are receiving frees us to function in a Godly way and introduces us to the reality of Mark 11: 24. What I am *desiring* is now what God wants and is easy to *believe* because I am *receiving* it from Him.

The Spirit of God in Romans 8: 27 goes on to say that what we are believing is being borne by the Spirit of God to Jesus at the right hand of God who according to Romans 8: 34 and Hebrews 7: 25 is interceding with the Father on our behalf. Matthew 7: 7 – 11 informs us that all of our seeking and knocking in prayer is being answered by God. We need to remember to thank Him for the answers He gives.[107]

"No" is not an answer to prayer! All true prayer originates with God not man's desires, no matter how good they may be; it must therefore be His will and "Yes" must be the answer.

So the process continues.

PRAYER DOESN'T CHANGE GOD'S MIND IT CHANGES YOU!

*"Now this is the confidence that we have in Him, that **if we ask anything according to His will,** He hears us."*[108] Asking according to His will comes first not last.

What is God's will for you? *"For whom He foreknew, He also predestined **to be conformed to the image of His Son.**"*[109]

*"In Him also **we have obtained an inheritance,** being predestined **according to the purpose of Him** who works all things according to the counsel of His will."*

God had everything worked out the way it should be before it was to happen. Do you expect to change God's mind and will by your prayers? Who will be changed by your prayers? God will not only cause you to pray according to what He wants, He will use you to bring it about. Real prayer can be the most exciting thing you will ever do!

"THERE'S ALWAYS A WAY WHEN YOU PRAY"

Chapter 9

THE KEY REVEALED

Meditation has always been a cornerstone of Christian growth and practise. The Monastic Movement, whose peak came in the fourth century AD, majored on it. Even the Jews were strong in their meditative practise.

The key to Christian meditation is found early in the book of Joshua. He sums up the teaching of his mentor, Moses in these words: *'This Book of the Law shall not depart from your mouth, but you shall meditate in it day and night, that you may observe to do according to all that is written in it. For then you will make your way prosperous, and then you will have good success."*[110]

THE KEY TO PROSPERITY AND SUCCESS IS MEDITATING ON THE WORD OF GOD

The Hebrew word for meditate meant *"to mutter or to utter."* *'This Book of the Law shall not depart from your mouth,"* means that it is the Word of God that must be muttered or uttered *"day and night."*

The purpose of meditation is to work out what God wants to do with his word. How are we to put it into practise? How is God going to involve us in his great plans for the universe? The outcome of meditation is so practical that it is no wonder there have been so many inventions and creative works achieved by Christians.

Andrew Murray is credited with defining meditation as *"holding the Word of God in your heart until it has affected every phase of your life."* It is contemplation with a view to application or thinking about doing. It is holding the Word of God up like a gem, looking at every gleaming facet, allowing the true value of its inherent worth to affect your every sense.

MEDITATION REQUIRES CHEWING, ANALYSING AND ACTION.

Meditation is chewing over the Word of God like a cow chews its cud. Processing spiritual food that renews your mind as it also accomplishes God's will. It is digesting the plans and promises of God.

The prophet Jeremiah was elated at the reality of this principle: *"Your words were found, and I ate them, And Your word was to me the joy and rejoicing of my heart; For I am called by Your name, O LORD God of hosts."*[111]

It is analysing its purposes, consequences and outcomes as a scientist would contemplate an experiment, allowing the Holy Spirit to release the hidden beauty and potential of his will. It is making plans to get it into productive action. It has often been said *"the road to hell is paved with good intentions."* It is also true that *"dreamers become what they dream."* Day dreamers never become anything.

Spiritual illumination without corresponding action is a sure way of drying up any spiritual life. We must make plans that have inbuilt checks to make sure that what is contemplated actually happens.

"Blessed is the man Who walks not in the counsel of the ungodly, Nor stands in the path of sinners, Nor sits in the seat of the scornful; But his delight is in the law of the LORD, And in His law he meditates day and night. He shall be like a tree Planted by the rivers of water, That brings forth its fruit in its season, Whose leaf also shall not wither; And whatever he does shall prosper."[112]

The promise of this Psalm is that meditation on the Word of God is like a tree with a permanent life source at its roots. Water is often used as a figure of the Holy Spirit (Jesus uses it this way in John 7: 37 – 39).

Meditation, therefore, will facilitate the operation of the Holy Spirit through a believer's life. Rather than opening one's spirit to the mystique of uncertain eastern religious technique, instead, by meditating on the word of God, open it to the miracle-working power of God's own Holy Spirit.

The result of Meditation on the Word will be production of fruit of the Spirit in the believers life. It will mean a new sustaining power and a new prosperity in every understanding. Meditation implants the Word of God into the soul and spirit of the Christian.

"Receive with meekness the implanted word, which is able to save your souls."[113]

"But he who looks into the perfect law of liberty (ie. Meditates on the Word – Ed) *and continues in it, and is not a forgetful hearer but a doer of the work, this one will be blessed in what he does."*[114]

THE PROMISES OF GOD

Among the promises that the Word of God offers for the true meditator are:

Obvious success – 1Timothy 4: 15
Prosperity – Psalm 1: 2 and 3
More wisdom than my teachers – Psalm 119: 99 and 100
Fullness of Joy – Psalm 63: 5 and 6
Victory over sin – Psalm 119: 9-11
Ability to give wise counsel – Proverbs 22: 17 and 18, 21

MEDITATION IS THE INVISIBLE LINK

The link between what God wants and what you do. The link between living on milk or living on solid food.[115] The link between existence and abundance, as the psalm writer says: *"My soul shall be satisfied as with marrow and fatness, And my mouth shall praise You with joyful lips. When I remember You on my bed, I meditate on You in the night watches."*[116]

"Muse" is the name of the statue of the thinker – we often see pictures of him sitting around in his stone splendour with his elbow on his knee and his chin in his hand. Add *"a"* to *"muse"* and we have the enemy of all meditation. When amusement comes before getting alone with God and paying the cost to find the will of God then we are on the beginning of a downhill slide.

We must also be aware of getting alone with our own thoughts instead of getting alone with God's thoughts. Active seeking is the answer to this; disciplined, active seeking, wanting to know with all the heart will overcome anything.

It is important that we personalise the Word of God when we meditate. Note how the Psalmist does exactly that in Psalm 19: 14:

> *"Let the words of my mouth and the meditation of my heart Be acceptable in Your sight, O LORD, my strength and my Redeemer."*

Obedience is also a key. If we are not prepared to obey what God says to us, then we cannot expect God to bother saying much. When we are willing to do whatever it is God says without question, then the experience of the Psalmist will excite us also: *"Oh, how I love Your law! It is my meditation all the day."*[117]

The apostle Paul found the secret: *"Let the word of Christ dwell in you richly in all wisdom, teaching and admonishing one another in psalms and hymns and spiritual songs, singing with grace in your hearts to the Lord."*[118]

King Solomon had already discovered it hundreds of years before: *"When you roam, they will lead you; When you sleep, they will keep you; And when you awake, they will speak with you. For the commandment is a lamp, And the law a light; Reproofs of instruction are the way of life,"*[119]

Meditation on the Word of God at the direction of the Spirit of God is the inevitable secret of the abundant Christian life!

PSEUDO MEDITATION

Meditation has become the buzz word of the modern era. University lecturers, business motivators, medical professionals trying to relieve stress and a host of lesser lights are all advocating meditation as the answer to modern day maladies and ego's.

Unfortunately, modern day problems are increasing at a much speedier tempo in spite of the meditative cure-alls. Suicide rates, divorce rates, homicides and the full gamut of stress- related diseases are all increasing alarmingly.

Modern day meditation and its associated new age mysticism is not really modern at all. Meditation, as it is now being taught, is only the old, multi-god, eastern religious meditation that has been around for thousands of years. This type of meditation has had more than enough time to demonstrate its ability to improve the lot of its adherents. In actual fact, it has done no such thing. The countries that have embraced such meditative practises have shown little ingenuity and progress apart from copying western trends. The lot of their people has been poverty stricken and socially downtrodden.

On the contrary, the countries that have, in the past, embraced Christianity have all demonstrated great creativity and social benefit. It is unfortunate that these countries are now turning from their birthright to embrace practises that can only be ultimately and eternally detrimental.

Not only has eastern meditation gained ground in the wider community but it has even penetrated the organised churches of western society. New teaching may now be found that is a combination of the many-god, eastern, mystical practise with mainline church teaching.

The apostle Paul warned: *"What am I saying then? That an idol is anything, or what is offered to idols is anything? Rather, that the things which the Gentiles sacrifice they sacrifice to demons and not to God, and I do not want you to have fellowship with demons."*[120] It is clear that idols were demonic representations. To be involved with such many-god, many-spirit, mysticism is to open oneself to deceptive, lying forces that are not only anti-Christian but also personally destructive.

The "mantra" is the core of eastern religion. This mind dulling, hypnotic, endlessly repetitive word is pure mysticism. It is usually a manifestation of the spirit of the idol to which it belongs. The requirement of emptying out the mind and trying to bypass it while the mantra is being droned is a sure way to open oneself to demonic forces.

The whole point of Christianity is to "renew the mind"[121] not to empty it out. *There is no biblical requirement to empty the mind or bypass it. Such teaching is anti-Christian and opposite to the historical and biblical norms of the Christian faith.*

To advance the idea that a mantra should be "amen" or "hallelujah" may not be quite the same as the explicit mantras of eastern mysticism but it is still leaving the passive mind open and susceptible to the imprint of wrong spiritual forces.

"Benefits" of eastern style meditation will be short lived. The question should be asked: *"Why bother with it when the Bible lays out clearly, and the Holy Spirit reinforces, the necessity of true meditation?"*

TRUE MEDITATION FILLS THE SOUL
WITH THE PRESENCE OF GOD

The whole idea that God is somewhere "out there" and we call Him in to help out occasionally may have been the way it went for the average Jewish person in the Old Testament era, but it was not what God desired for them. *"I call to remembrance my song in the night; I meditate within my heart, And my spirit makes diligent search,"* [122] said the Psalmist. This is what God wanted for every person but it took the crucifixion of Jesus and the release of the Holy Spirit to bring it to reality for the Christian.

When we want to focus on our Father we can release His Spirit within. Start out singing then continue meditating on the Word. Our meditation is not relying on a God out there to fill a vacancy, instead our minds and emotions are reaching into the abiding Spirit within and drawing out the divine presence He has put there. This is being empowered in our meditation by the very presence of Jesus flowing into our mind, emotion and will. *But God has revealed (things He has prepared for those who love Him[123]) to us through His Spirit. For the Spirit searches all things, yes, the deep things of God.* [124]

Now He who searches the hearts knows what the mind of the Spirit is, because He makes intercession for the saints according to the will of God.[125]

When true meditation takes place it is a two-way experience. The Holy Spirit within works with our meditation and intercedes with the Father, God and communicates with us by revelation. We are assured God is hearing our intercession as we enjoy our relationship with Him and His joy flows thru' us.

There is much room for researching meditation on the Word of God especially when we know we have willing associates in the Godhead to share with. The results will be life-changing.

Chapter 10

IMPLANTING THE KEY

THE WORD OF GOD WILL ACCMPLISH
THE PURPOSES OF GOD

We have already established the need to meditate on the Word of God (Chapter 9). This is not just a nice intellectual exercise which makes us feel good; we need to build it into our lives so it impels us automatically into the will of God. James, half brother of Jesus, says: *So get rid of all uncleanness and the rampant outgrowth of wickedness, and in a humble (gentle, modest) spirit receive and welcome the Word which implanted and rooted [in your hearts] contains the power to save your souls.*[126]

When we welcome Jesus (the living Word) into our lives we need to implant (engraft[127]) Him into our heart so building the reality of the salvation in soul and spirit. We need the written Word of God released within. James assures us that we not only need the written word but we need to do what that Word says.[128]

We have all seen people make a profession of faith in Jesus and next week they have forgotten all about it. The Word needs to be implanted in them.

If you have got this far into the book you have already been introduced to verse analysis (Chapter 7). But this is only a step along the way. Journaling is the decisive method of developing your relationship with God. For this you need a notebook in which you will record whatever it is you feel God is saying to you and what you are going to do about it. In one local Church I was involved with, children are taught to successfully journal so you can do it too.

First: look for what you think God is saying to you!

Second: analyse the segment God has given you. Break it into its natural parts.

From your experience of verse analysis you will have already checked the context of the passage you are considering. Let's take the verse from James, quoted above and break it into its natural parts. This is quoted from the Amplified Bible so a great amount of the work needed is already done for you.

So get rid of all uncleanness and the rampant outgrowth of wickedness, and in a humble (gentle, modest) spirit receive and welcome the Word which implanted and rooted [in your hearts] contains the power to save your souls.- James 1:21

1. *So get rid of all uncleanness and the rampant outgrowth of wickedness*

   PARAPHRASE: Remove from my being anything that could be construed to be dirty and get up other peoples noses.

   ASK yourself: what things do I do that could be deemed unclean and thereby wrongly influence my family? What things do I do in my work or business that could be classed as wicked and thereby wrongly pressure my associates?

2. *in a humble (gentle, modest) spirit*

   PARAPHRASE: Let my fortitude be unassuming, calm and reticent within.

   ASK: how do I come across to others? Is it in a form of superior self-righteousness? If so I ask God to teach me humility. No matter where I'm at I need more of this.

3. *Receive and welcome the Word*

   PARAPHRASE: accept and hail God's instructions

ASK: Am I hungry for what God wants for me? *Blessed are those who hunger and thirst for righteousness, For they shall be filled.*[129] Do I welcome things God is wanting of me or do I just grudgingly go along with them? If I can't welcome them openly I won't receive them, instead, they will just be surface things that will float off and never become *implanted.*

4. *the Word which implanted and rooted [in your hearts] contains the power...*

PARAPHRASE: what God says must be engrafted and sincerely planted within my personality because it has inherent authority

ASK: How can I implant (or engraft) the Word into my heart? Answer: Meditate on it; memorize it; share it; pray it into existence; do it; release the latent power now available within.

5. *contains the power to save your souls.*

Rejoice in the salvation God has given me. The salvation I experienced when I first received Jesus; salvation, presently happening to me as I continue to live the spirit-filled life; salvation, assured by the Holy Spirit, when I go to be with the Father in my ultimate home in heaven.

The power of God will not be released to someone who just wishes God would do it. It has to be worked into life. If the word of God is *"living and active and sharp"*[130] we must allow it to till the soil of our souls to let grow what has been planted in our spirit. We have to free things up so the activity of what is growing can have full liberty to be itself. Sharp, root-pruning tools, must cut away the impediments in the roots and the soil, allowing the fruit-bearing seed in our spirit, much of which may have lain inactive for a long period, to bring forth the fruit God wants.[131]

When you are reading a narrative passage, a story, a parable or some prophetic statement, try to picture what you are reading in your mind.

Try to live it yourself. Check up on what you feel about it. Who do you identify with in the storyline? What is God saying and what are you going to do about it? Are there particular steps you must now take as a result of what you have just experienced?

Now you find a verse somewhere in the Bible and have a go! Try and find a verse to memorize.When you have been doing this for some time you will have a record of what God has said enabling you to look back and refresh the things God has said to you.

SCRIPTURE MEMORY IS FOR EVERYONE

Most of us would claim to have poor memories. In spite of this we usually manage to reel off countless facts and figures that relate to our job, our favourite sport or our special hobby. What we retain in our memories is obviously influenced by its importance to us. **Our level of interest or need can generate mental capacity we didn't know existed.**

There is a great necessity to learn the word of God by heart. **A time is coming when the Scripture will not be readily available.** When that time comes (it already has in some countries) only what we have stored up will be available to us and to those to whom we minister.

Not only is the Word of God to be stored up for the future it is profitable right now. *"Your word I have hidden in my heart, That I might not sin against You."*[132] *"Keep your heart with all diligence, For out of it spring the issues of life."*[133] **Knowing the Word of God intimately will produce Holy Spirit power in our lives that will effect every goal, task and issue of our existence.**

Many modern day business men and women are taking courses in how to develop good memory. These leaders of business see great benefit in being able to commit things reliably to their mind and are prepared to pay great amounts of money to learn how. The attitude of wanting to memorize key details is the answer.

If the desire is there anything can be done!

For the Christian there is great assistance in memorizing Scripture. The Holy Spirit is more than willing to help. He will impress God's revelation on our hearts and illumine that inspiration to our minds.

This does not eliminate the work necessary to commit a text to memory but it does promise Divine help and blessing in our labour.

Being obedient to God's Word is the guarantee of Holy Spirit help and blessing. *"And these words which I command you today shall be in your heart."*[134] The outcome of obedience to this verse is contained in another: *"Let the word of Christ dwell in you richly in all wisdom,"* [135] A sense of richness and previously unknown wisdom will be ours as a result of memorizing God's Word. Couple this with Philippians 4: 13 *"I can do all things through Christ who strengthens me."* and we can have the confidence of both God's help and His blessing.

MULTI-VITAMIN

Jesus said: *"MAN SHALL NOT LIVE BY BREAD ALONE, BUT BY EVERY WORD THAT PROCEEDS FROM THE MOUTH OF GOD."*[136] Since eating bread is likened to feeding on the Word of God, memorizing scripture can readily be likened to taking vitamins. It's medicine and nourishment for the soul. *"As newborn babes, desire the pure milk of the word, that you may grow thereby,"* [137]

A fit body is one of the modern rages. An unfit soul (especially in the Church) is one of the modern blights. Memorizing Scripture helps keep you spiritually fit and vital. It sharpens up the double-edged Sword of the Spirit[138] within. It vitamises the soul to go on the offensive over the pressures and demands of this modern life.

MEMORIZING SCRIPTURE WILL GIVE YOU...

...confidence in witnessing. When you don't know what to say, God can release from the storehouse of your soul the vital morsel that the person to whom you are speaking so desperately needs – it might be the word that changes their life. When you have key verses memorized there is direction in what you say and what to do – no more uncertainty or procrastination. It's the difference between being an ineffectual onlooker or a vital soulwinner.

...triumph over worry. If you don't really know the Word of God then as Jesus said *"the worries of the world ... enter in and choke the Word, and it becomes unfruitful.*[139] Spiritual life becomes dry and dreary.

No matter what uncertainty of the future or spectre from the past comes against you, **when you write the Word of God on your heart you can experience God's perfect peace.** When you really know it, God's Word is *"quick and powerful"* it will pierce any intruding *"thought or intention".*[140] It will keep your mind renewed and fixed on the Father.

> **...victory over sin.** Someone has said: *God's Word will keep you from sin or sin will keep you from God's Word."* It's true! No matter what your besetting sin if you regularly memorize appropriate scriptures you are giving the Holy Spirit a special chance to set you free.

Modern computer usage has coined the phrase: *"Garbage in garbage out."* It's correct for the human life also-we become what we take in. If we continually take in the word of God that is what will be assimilated into our system and that is what will eventually come out.

DAILY VICTORY

The prophet Jeremiah demonstrates this principle, when, in the midst of his worst predicament, down in the miry hole, he says: *Your words were found, and I ate them, And Your word was to me the joy and rejoicing of my heart; For I am called by Your name, O LORD God of hosts.*[141]

King David also found the secret. *Your word I have hidden in my heart, That I might not sin against You.*[142] Thousands of Christians have found memorizing scripture is a key to daily victory. You can too. It will equip you to meet all future needs and opportunities.

Chapter 11

EXPANDING RELATIONSHIPS

In response to the questioning of the Jewish leaders Jesus offered these words: *"The first of all the commandments is: 'HEAR, O ISRAEL, THE LORD OUR GOD, THE LORD IS ONE. AND YOU SHALL LOVE THE LORD YOUR GOD WITH ALL YOUR HEART, WITH ALL YOUR SOUL, WITH ALL YOUR MIND, AND WITH ALL YOUR STRENGTH.' This is the first commandment. And the second, like it, is this: 'YOU SHALL LOVE YOUR NEIGHBOR AS YOURSELF.' There is no other commandment greater than these."*[143]

In previous chapters the relationship between you and Jesus has been emphasised, but, as you can see if the successive second commandment is really happening it is going to involve other people.

Our educational systems have helped us and our ego's have responded in a critical display of self-centeredness requiring relationships that add something to enlarge our own persona. Jesus was of the view that we look to what we can do to positively engage the lives of others with no thought of personal gain (not even kudos that we have someone who wants to hear from us). This is loving the Jesus way – the best for others that ultimately will draw from us the best of the life being given by the Holy Spirit of God

THE JESUS PRIORITIES

One of the great things about Jesus was his ability to live what he taught. It's all summarised in John 15 verse 13:*" Greater love has no one than this, than to lay down one's life for his friends."*After saying this he went out and demonstrated it on the cross at Calvary. Following his resurrection he didn't start a gossip session with his disciples about the wrong that had been done to him or the lack of back-up from His disciples. Jesus was so refreshingly different. He didn't slam the high priests, deliver poisonous barbs against Pilate, lampoon the fickle populace who had quickly changed from adulation to denunciation or any other negative thing. His attitude was focused on the future of building his Church. No retribution, only love for the world – very different to our human attitudes.

Jesus aim was encapsulated when he said: ***"I will build my church"!***[144]

How is he going to do it?

Answer: thru' you and me! By forgiving and keeping on forgiving all those who sin against us.[145] (especially those who just ignore us).

JESUS IS BUILDING HIS BODY

In Ephesians 4 verse 11 it says: *And He Himself gave some to be apostles, some prophets, some evangelists, and some pastors and teachers,* these are, as John Maxwell says: *to hold you accountable and act as your "alarm bells."*[146] In other words to keep us honest as they are*" equipping the saints* [that's us] *for the work of ministry, for the edifying of the body of Christ,* (verse 12).

Unfortunately we can find many people claiming to be Christians who are not responsible to anyone except themselves and despite assertions of "ministry" to others, are not contributing to building up the Body of Christ at all. The best they can do is produce a form of spiritual anarchy.

How do we know who Jesus has given for these offices? We can know by the obvious evidence of their calling and the recognition of the individual gift by others with the same gift. Beyond this there are many other gifts in the Body of Christ, you have some of them, they all need to be enlisted and used for the edifying of the Body of Christ. All are different but all just as valuable as one another.

Obey those who rule over you, and be submissive, for they watch out for your souls, as those who must give account. Let them do so with joy and not with grief, for that would be unprofitable for you.[147]

THE BODY IS A FELLOWSHIP

Not just a talk-fest or reminiscence, it is a proactive force based on a relationship with Jesus.

That which was from the beginning, which we have heard, which we have seen with our eyes, which we have looked upon, and our hands have handled, concerning the Word of life—the life was manifested, and we have seen, and bear witness, and declare to you that eternal life which was with the Father and was manifested to us—that which we have seen and heard we declare to you, that you also may have fellowship with us; and truly our fellowship is with the Father and with His Son Jesus Christ. And these things we write to you that your joy may be full.[148]

The late Dr J Sidlow Baxter defined Fellowship as: *"The common sharing of the sacred secret."* [149]

The Church is an interrelated entity made up of various different human parts bound together by Jesus *"from whom the whole body, joined and knit together by what every joint supplies, according to the effective working by which every part does its share, causes growth of the body for the edifying of itself in love.*[150]

Notice every member of the fellowship must be *joined*, not just have their name added to a church roll but actually closely knit to someone else in the Body. From this *joining* you will together be able to draw from the Holy Spirit and supply that which the Body needs to grow, sharing with the others in the Body and demonstrating the love of God.

This is the purpose of the leadership giftings spoken of above: *"for the equipping of the saints for the work of ministry, for the edifying of the body of Christ, till we all come to the unity of the faith and of the knowledge of the Son of God, to a perfect man, to the measure of the stature of the fullness of Christ."*[151]

To get to this stage requires a lot of forgiving, a lot of love, a lot of persistence, a lot of non-judgement - all available thru' Jesus. We may not be aware immediately of the contribution we are making in joining with others but it becomes obvious as we see the Church becoming humbler, healthier, prospering, growing in grace and enlarging.

THE BODY IS A CORPORATE
WORSHIPPING ORGANISM

The book of Hebrews, right from chapter 1, is about promoting the excellence of the person & ministry of our great high priest, Jesus Christ. There are many themes in the Book of Hebrews; among them are the themes of Sacrifice, Priestly Ministry, Worship and Sanctuary.

'For the law appoints as high priests men who have weakness, but the word of the oath, which came after the law, appoints the Son who has been perfected forever."[152]

In declaring Jesus High Priestly Ministry, Hebrews chapter eight verse one goes on to say: *"Now this is the main point."* So: -

Let the main point be the main point.

Verses one and two continue:*"we have such a high priest, who has taken His seat at the right hand of the throne of the Majesty in the heavens, a minister in the sanctuary and in the true tabernacle, which the Lord pitched, not man."*

Verse five goes on to tell us that this heavenly sanctuary had an earthly *copy & shadow* and it tells us that Moses had Divine instruction when he built the Tabernacle and he ensured it was built according to that instruction. The Tabernacle of the Old Testament was an earthly copy of the heavenly sanctuary now with Jesus as the High Priest. Our task is to enter that spiritual sanctuary, worshiping Him *in Spirit and truth* [153] not in Jewish legality. When we gather we should enter into that heavenly sanctuary. This we can do when we learn to offer ourselves, body, soul and spirit to our Lord and enjoy the relationship together with Him and our fellow saints.

THE BODY IS A SERVING MEDIUM

"Whoever desires to become great among you, let him be your servant. And whoever desires to be first among you, let him be your slave— just as the Son of Man did not come to be served, but to serve, and to give His life a ransom for many."[154]

"But he who is greatest among you shall be your servant. And whoever exalts himself will be humbled, and he who humbles himself will be exalted."[155]

These are the words of Jesus. As you have already read above there are special ministry gifts but Jesus is clearly spelling things out here. Greater than all of these is the gift given to every Christian - the gift of serving![156]

How can we be effectively joined to another and bring about growth – by loving them and serving them? *"For you, brethren, have been called to liberty; only do not use liberty as an opportunity for the flesh, but through love serve one another."* [157]

There are three things that will cause the community to take notice of the Church?

1. Our love for each other within the Church. *A new commandment I give to you, that you love one another; as I have loved you, that you also love one another. By this all will know that you are My disciples, if you have love for one another."*[158]

2. Our willingness to serve others, regardless of who they are, as Jesus charged: *"If anyone desires to be first, he shall be last of all and servant of all."*[159]

3. A healthy relationship with the Holy Spirit, allowing him to do his best work in revealing Jesus[160] and supplying the oil[161] which enables the Body to function smoothly fulfilling 1. And 2. Above.

THIS IS THE BODY!

The Body of Christ is not one denomination; it is all of them who are true to the Gospel of Christ. All those who have been born of the Spirit of God from time immemorial to those yet to find the reality of Christ comprise the ultimate Church.

I, [Paul] therefore, the prisoner of the Lord, beseech you to walk worthy of the calling with which you were called, with all lowliness and gentleness, with longsuffering, bearing with one another in love, endeavouring to keep the unity of the Spirit in the bond of peace. There is one body and one Spirit, just as you were called in one hope of your calling; one Lord, one faith, one baptism; one God and Father of all, who is above all, and through all, and in you all. But to each one of us grace was given according to the measure of Christ's gift.[162]

BODY CHECK-LIST

1. Are we *"walking* [living] *worthily of the calling with which we were called?"*
2. Are we living in*" all lowliness and gentleness"* or are we living in the pride of past history or current superior knowledge?
3. Are we *"longsuffering"* under real persecution or are we suffering long in the apparent dilemma of things people have said or done in the past, failing to release true forgiveness?
4. *"Bearing with one another in love,"* positively being the answer for people who, at that point, can't do it for themselves.
5. Are we *"endeavouring to keep the unity of the Spirit in the bond of peace?"* Jesus didn't say blessed are the peace lovers, he said: *"Blessed are the peacemakers!"*[163] It takes some effort to maintain peaceful unity. How are we doing with this?
6. Are we using the grace gifts given to us to honour our one Lord and his Body?

Chapter 12

THE PARACLETE

Jesus was the greatest example of a human being that has ever existed. The appointment of the Holy Spirit accurately declared Him portraying His complete experience of human life and accurately revealing the totality of His divine nature.

A child, born in an obscure village, He grew up in another obscure village in an equally obscure corner of the world. He worked in a carpenter shop until he was 30. Then, for 3 ½ years he was an itinerant preacher.

He never wrote a book. He never held an office. He never owned a home. He never had a family. He never went to college. He never set foot inside a big city. He never travelled more than two hundred miles from where he was born, yet His testimony has gone around the world. He never did any of the things that usually accompany greatness. He had no wealth or influence. He had no credentials but Himself. He had nothing to do with this world except the naked power of His divine manhood.

While still a young man, the tide of public opinion turned against Him. He was turned over to His enemies. He went through a mockery of a trial. He was crucified between two thieves. His executioners gambled for the only piece of property he had, while He was dying, and that was His robe. When He was dead, He was taken down and laid in a borrowed tomb, through the pity of a friend.

In infancy He startled a king; in boyhood He puzzled the wise men; in manhood ruled the course of nature. He healed the multitudes without medicine, and made no charges for His services. He never wrote a book, yet all the libraries of the country could not hold the books that have been written about Him. He never wrote a song, yet He has furnished the theme of more songs than all the song writers combined. He never founded a college, yet all the schools together cannot boast as many students as He has. He never practised psychiatry and yet He has healed more broken hearts than doctors have healed broken bodies.

He is the star of astronomy, the rock of geology, the lion and the lamb of zoology, the harmoniser of all discords and the healer of all diseases. Great men have come and gone, yet He lives on. Herod could not kill Him, satan could not seduce Him, death could not destroy Him, the grave could not hold Him.

He never marshalled an army, drafted a soldier, nor fired a gun, yet no leader ever mobilised more volunteers. He had a public ministry of only 3 ½ years, yet here we are, billions of people, 2000 years later, saying "Jesus, you are wonderful," because He is.

To explain Jesus Christ is impossible; to ignore Him is disastrous; to reject Him is fatal. Human speech is too limited to describe Him, the human mind too small to comprehend Him, and the human heart can never completely absorb who Jesus Christ is. To know Him is to love Him. To love Him is to trust Him. To trust Him is to be radically, dramatically and eternally transformed.

Twenty centuries have come and gone and today He is the centrepiece of the human race and the leader of the column of human progress. All the armies that ever marched and all the navies that ever sailed, all the parliaments that ever sat, all the kings that have ever reigned, put together have not affected the life of mankind upon this earth as powerfully as that one solitary life; Jesus the Messiah.[164]

When He breathed on His disciples and said: *"Receive the Holy Spirit."*[165] They were receiving all that is spoken of above into their lives and so are we when we receive the Holy Spirit into our lives. Here is the Holy Spirit doing His best work – intimately revealing Jesus.[166]

Jesus was not just an example He became a living legacy thru' the Holy Spirit which He gave. We can look back at the things Jesus said & did but he didn't just leave it at that, he gave us the ability to live those things thru' the Holy Spirit *"I will pray the Father, and He will give you another Helper, that He may abide with you forever"* said Jesus. This Holy Spirit is someone we should come to know because He will be with us FOREVER.

We need to prove His assets rather than bypass His existence figuring on using the Word, the Church or the example of Jesus instead, failing to consider His imputed life.

This *other helper* is the Paraclete (Greek: Parakletos) the one of the same genus[167] as the Father and the Son, with the same personal attributes, commissioned to help, console, comfort, counsel, intercede and advocate[168] for us. He is a spiritual comforter enabling us to cope spiritually, mentally, emotionally as well as physically with trauma's that continually beset us.

This paraclete word is used five times in the New Testament, four times of the Holy Spirit and once of Jesus. His presence for all of us is anticipated in the Old Testament. Ezekiel says of God: *"I will put My Spirit in you, and you shall live,"*[169] Jeremiah echoes the same thought: *"But this is the covenant that I will make ... I will put My law in their minds, and write it on their hearts; and I will be their God, and they shall be My people."*[170] Joel is even more specific: *"And it shall come to pass afterward that I will pour out My Spirit on all flesh."*[171]

John the Baptist foreshadows Jesus releasing the Holy Spirit to His disciples. *"He who is coming after me is mightier than I, ... He will baptise* [immerse - Ed] *you with the Holy Spirit and fire."*[172]

Jesus Himself foretold the coming of the Holy Spirit for everyone, not just for prophets and special leaders as in the Old Testament. *On the last day, that great day of the feast, Jesus stood and cried out, saying, "If anyone thirsts, let him come to Me and drink. He who believes in Me, as the Scripture has said, out of his heart will flow rivers of living water." But this He spoke concerning the Spirit, whom those believing in Him would receive; for the Holy Spirit was not yet given, because Jesus was not yet glorified.* [173]

The *Great Day* followed the Feast of Tabernacles. For seven days the people lived in their temporary booths around Jerusalem celebrating the gift of the land God had given them. Water had been taken daily from the Pool of Siloam and poured out in the Temple recounting the way Moses had struck the rock and given water to the people[174] as they traversed the wilderness during their 40 year journey from Egypt to the Promised Land. The eighth day of the Feast charged the people to take what had been given back to their homes and bless all those around them. Jesus is now using the symbolism of the water pouring as a foretaste of what was to come – the release of the Spirit of God.

Jesus gives a condition for knowing the Holy Spirit. *"If you love Me, keep My commandments. And I will pray the Father, and He will give you another Helper, that He may abide with you forever."*[175] If we love Jesus we will have this helper/advocate abiding (living) within us, always ready for us to relate with at any time about any problem or blessing. If we only have keeping Jesus commandments as an option then the paraclete/counsellor will not be abiding or doing anything useful.

Jesus gives definition to the Holy Spirit in the following verse: *"the Spirit of truth, whom the world cannot receive, because it neither sees Him nor knows Him; but you know Him, for He dwells with you and will be in you."*[176] The Spirit of heavenly reality the world doesn't want to know is Jesus, He is standing before them. He said, you can see this Spirit standing before you. Very soon, when I go to be with the Father, you will be born of the Spirit and He will be in you. I won't leave you by yourself. I won't leave you an orphan.[177]

Jesus teaches us how to know Him: *But the Helper, the Holy Spirit, whom the Father will send in My name, He will teach you all things, and bring to your remembrance all things that I said to you.*[178] This seems to be the principle forgotten by most Christians. School taught us to learn thru' our minds – learning from the outside. This means we don't naturally look to learn from the inside. If we want to know about the real character of Jesus we need to talk to the one who will bring to remembrance of what He has said.

We need this to happen continually as Jesus explains in John chapter 15 where He urges us to live in this principle (see Chapter 5).[179]

THE ADVANTAGE

We would all like to have Jesus around in the flesh but, if we did, we would not be able to have the Holy Spirit within us which is far better. If Jesus were physically here He would be located in one place at a time. As the Holy Spirit, He can be everywhere at once especially within every true Christian. *Nevertheless I tell you the truth. It is to your advantage that I go away; for if I do not go away, the Helper will not come to you; but if I depart, I will send Him to you.*[180]

Jesus has commissioned the Holy Spirit to do some basic things. His job is to bring conviction! This is not the same as condemnation. Conviction has to do with the intimate personal relationship between you and God. It has nothing to do with anyone else (altho' it may have some results that will affect someone else even tho' they might not know what has happened to you). It has nothing to do with shame (altho' it may release personal guilt from within you). As time goes by you will discover this Holy Spirit convicting power can lead you away from unhealthy negative things and into sound positive things. It doesn't matter what other people say about you (condemnation), it only matters what God thinks and that's between you and Him.

And when He has come, He will convict the world of sin, and of righteousness, and of judgment: of sin, because they do not believe in Me; of righteousness, because I go to My Father and you see Me no more; of judgment, because the ruler of this world is judged.[181]

Conviction of sin is nothing to worry about. Facing up to our personal history and whatever we have done wrong in the past enables faith in Jesus to clean us up and replace the sin with His love, joy and peace. To think this is just a theory or a theology is to miss the point. Jesus wants to impart real love, real joy and real peace you can experience now. It can happen to you, as it has for millions of others, if your belief is sincere and thorough.

Jesus wants us to be righteous – not self righteous. This is not a popular concept in the 21st Century; actually it has never ever been popular. We tend to judge people by the good things they do, the motive behind what they do is not considered. The apostle Paul gets it right when he says: *For scarcely for a righteous man will one die; yet perhaps for a good man someone would even dare to die.*[182] God is more interested in what's inside of us.

If we have right thinking and right motivation it will automatically come out right. Fruit of the Spirit[183] will involuntarily flow from us, producing healthy attitude and outlook.

We can safely leave any judgement to God, He knows who to blame for the troubles that beset this world. The devil knows that ultimately he is beaten.

Before Jesus left this world he said*: you shall receive power when the Holy Spirit has come upon you;*[184] and we still will!

Chapter 13

THE POWER

Dr Billy Graham, the finest Christian statesman the 20th century produced, stated:

> *"Man has two great spiritual needs. One is for forgiveness. The other is for goodness."*
>
> *"God heard that first cry for help, that cry for forgiveness, and answered it at Calvary."*
>
> *But God also heard our second cry, that cry for goodness, and answered it at Pentecost."* [185]

The goodness of God is what this world needs. Not just good things, particularly those done for personal aggrandisement, but goodness coming from a just and merciful heart. *He has shown you, O man, what is good; And what does the LORD require of you But to do justly, To love mercy, And to walk humbly with your God?*[186]

It would be really difficult to produce goodness, justice, mercy and humility if it weren't for the active presence of God in our lives thru' the Holy Spirit. *Or do you despise the riches of His goodness, forbearance, and longsuffering, not knowing that the goodness of God leads you to repentance?*[187]

The goodness, justice, mercy and humility of God are not placid things. Jesus said: *"You shall receive power when the Holy Spirit has come upon you."*[188]

Initially when He said this He was referring to His disciples witnessing to His character across the world. He promised to make the power of His personality obvious to His followers with a standout experience in their lives, something that would be obvious both to them and to those around and about them, something that would demonstrate the goodness of God.

When the day of Pentecost, following Jesus resurrection, came there were already those who had been impacted by His "born again" teaching[189] plus those who had otherwise received His Spirit.[190] Now John the Baptist's prophecy[191] about Him was coming to pass. Jesus picked this up in His valedictory speech to His disciples before He left them. *Wait for **the Promise** of the Father, "which," He said, "you have heard from Me; for John truly baptized with water, **but you shall be baptized with the Holy Spirit not many days from now.**"* [192]

"WHEN THE DAY OF PENTECOST HAD FULLY COME"[193]

It was not just the consciousness of a special day celebrating the historic arrival of the Children of Israel into their new land or a celebration of an abundant harvest; it was a declaration of God's intent to bequeath to His people a new and powerful determinate that would declare the reality of the work His son had achieved. For some people it is just an historical event and the Holy Spirit a fact of life with little substantial effect now. The detail of Jesus achievement on the cross mainly being an intellectual understanding.

That Day of Pentecost came with such a resonating impact it was not long before it was heard right across the world.[194] This promised baptism of the Holy Spirit prophetically reverberating from John the Baptist, was here! *This Jesus God has raised up, of which we are all witnesses. Therefore being exalted to the right hand of God, and having received from the Father **the promise** of the Holy Spirit, He poured out this which you now see and hear.*[195]

What they were seeing and hearing was for everyone for all time. *For **the promise** is to you and to your children, and to all who are afar off, as many as the Lord our God will call."*[196]

The 120 disciples[197] gathered in that upper room were suddenly confronted by strange odd phenomena.[198] Under ordinary circumstances it would have repelled them, their conservative culture would have cried out against such bizarre behaviour. But these people, now in a leaderless, indeterminate state, not knowing what was going to happen, praying, waiting on God as Jesus had instructed them,[199] exercising faith in His last words, were expecting the creative presence of the recently received Holy Spirit to lead them into whatever it was that Jesus said He would baptise them into.[200]

Picture this disparate group of people, fearful of the authorities, both Roman and Jewish, huddled together in a crowded upper room, in this no-account tiny place on the extremities of the far flung Roman Empire, with only the common experience of their now departed leader binding them together. Hidden away from the fiercely aggressive religious opposition who would dispatch them to the grave at a moments notice; now, expecting that the God of creation was going to do something extraordinary they had never experienced before; they released all the faith they had.

Today we are beginning to huddle together also. The constant anti-God pressure of the media and the obvious much publicised mistakes of the established church are pushing us into the same need of the early disciples. We need an engagement in the Holy Spirit that will declare the power, goodness, justice, mercy, humility and the grace of the Lord Jesus Christ just as the first disciples did.

WHAT DID THEY "SEE AND HEAR"?

What do you see and hear in the usual 21st century prayer meeting? Some one makes a formal speech to God about something – silence – another unrelated speech – more silence – another speech – much more silence and so on. Nothing like the prayer meeting of the early Church recorded in Acts chapter two. They had spent ten days getting themselves *"in one accord."*[201] Seeking whatever it was that Jesus wanted for them when He had told them to wait for the promise; unknowing what that would be but yet confident of the Holy Spirit among them.

All of a sudden, right on the prophetic cue of Pentecost, there was the sound of a mighty wind,[202] the sound you would hear as the wind howled and bent over the trees around; a sound obviously from heaven because it was only sound. It was heard by the neighbours and those in the street. Inside the room tongues of fire appeared above all the occupants of the room.[203]

And they were all filled with the Holy Spirit and began to speak with other tongues, as the Spirit gave them utterance.[204]

How did they know they were filled with the Holy Spirit? It was because the Spirit was doing in them something they couldn't do for themselves and the result was an edification of Jesus and the goodness of God within each life. They were taken over by the Holy Spirit and he was verbalising from deep within them. Nowhere in the scripture is a first person account given of: "I am filled (baptised) of/in /with the Holy Spirit and it's like this." Always it is a third person account" "This person is filled with the Spirit because I see God doing something these people couldn't do for themselves."

If the disciples were hiding away from the authorities they had really blown it now. As they burst out of that upper room the clamour of 120 people all speaking boldly, in what appeared to be a myriad of languages, had really exposed them. Because of the Feast there were people from all over the world around them. The miracle of the Spiritual outpouring took on another turn, it ceased to be just a miracle of personal experiences it became a miracle of hearing. It was not a matter of the 120 speaking particular languages, if so all of the 17 nations, spoken of in verses 5 – 11.would have needed to gather together in different places to hear their particular dialect, rather everyone heard it in their own language wherever they were.

Most people were flabbergasted and dumfounded trying to work out what was going on.[205] But the usual cynics were in evidence – "argh, their just drunk"[206] - a bit problematic for so many at 9 o'clock in the morning – were the taverns even open then?[207]

What they were seeing and hearing was an inauguration of the release of the empowering Spirit to anyone who heard the call of Jesus anywhere in the world. It fulfilled the Old Testament prophecy of Joel[208] and it would go on until the return of Jesus[209]

That day 3,000 heard the call and were baptised.[210] A few days later the number of men came to be 5,000,[211] (add in women and children and the company would probably have exceeded 15,000[212] - always more women in religious meetings).

THE HOLY SPIRIT GOES VIRAL

With the curb of constraint from Jewish nationalism gone[213] the soaring conversion rate quickly embraced the Gentiles (non-Jews).

Philip, the servant[214] turned evangelist, went down to the much despised Jewish half brothers and sisters in the city of Samaria and preached Christ to them.[215] *And the multitudes with one accord heeded the things spoken by Philip, hearing and seeing the miracles which he did. For unclean spirits, crying with a loud voice, came out of many who were possessed; and many who were paralyzed and lame were healed. And there was great joy in that city.*[216]

There certainly was great joy and great faith in Jesus in Samaria but no observable evidence that the Holy Spirit had been given them.[217] The apostles in Jerusalem heard about this, came down to Samaria laid hands upon everyone and they all began to demonstrate the Holy Spirit in their lives.[218] The goodness and grace of the Holy Spirit protected these new disciples. When Simon the sorcerer tried to gain kudos out of this, offering money so he could disseminate the Spirit as the apostles had, he was rebuffed sternly.[219]

On another occasion, miraculously, the Apostle Peter was called by the Spirit of God to Caesarea.[220] Following a Gospel presentation to a group of mainly Roman citizens[221] the Holy Spirit broke out on them, almost uninvited, and they all spoke in other tongues. Peter's assessment to the Apostles in Jerusalem sealed it: *And as I began to speak, the Holy Spirit fell upon them, as upon us at the beginning. Then I remembered the word of the Lord, how He said, 'John indeed baptized with water, but you shall be baptized with the Holy Spirit.' If therefore God gave them the same gift as He gave us when we believed on the Lord Jesus Christ, who was I that I could withstand God?"* [222] The Apostolic Council agreed – The fullness of the Holy Spirit had been given to all the world.[223]

More evidence of this came thru' the apostle Paul *"being sent out by the Holy Spirit"*[224] an action confirmed by the prophetic oversight of the Church in Caesarea.[225] He went specifically to the Gentiles. In Acts 19 it is reported he found some confessing disciples in Ephesus.[226]

The first thing he wanted to know was: *"Did you receive the Holy Spirit when you believed?"* [227] The response he received told him they didn't know there was a Holy Spirit, all they knew had come from John the Baptist.[228] Upon hearing the full Gospel the 12 men were baptised in the name of Jesus. Paul laid his hands on them and they spoke in other tongues and prophesied[229]. The Holy Spirit had arrived.

To be baptised in the Spirit yourself – seek it[230]. Ask your Pastor or other spiritual leader to lay hands on you and pray for you. Speaking in tongues is the most common sign of the presence of the Spirit of God within but there are many other gifts that can come with it. First Corinthians 12: 7 – 11 gives a list of potential gifts (Charismata[231]) the Spirit can empower thru' you. The following two chapters (13 and 14) give some instruction about how these gifts can be used in the Church. 1 Corinthians 1: 7 assures us *"that you come short in no gift* (charismata), *eagerly waiting for the revelation of our Lord Jesus Christ."* So between now and the time Jesus returns you will have whatever spiritual giftings you were designed to have, made available to you.

WHAT DO WE DO NOW?

Being baptised in the Holy Spirit is not an end in itself. It is not given so you can get power-drunk nor is it there so you can say 'I've got it - I'm a member of the club,' I don't need to do any more.' It's a beginning not an end.

Usually when someone is baptised in the Spirit it brings about a great enthusiasm for the things of God. That enthusiasm needs to be channelled into productive ministry for the Kingdom of God. To not do so will mean an eventual attrition to a point of neglect.

With *speaking in tongues* it is sometimes disregarded because the words being spoken are not understood,[232] particularly by other people. But they should, at least, edify the speaker.[233] Because each individual is an undivided being the vocal spiritual gift can be directed by a cooperative mind into any situation needing prayer. Using this charismatic gift can therefore release the Spirit directly from God to the point of need. Unfortunately, some people become dull in their personal spiritual life and "speaking in tongues" ceases to be a live vital spiritual thing; it becomes merely the mind and the emotions duplicating what they had previously learned from the Spirit. This is just the same as any usual idle gossip.[234] Attention must therefore be given by the speaker to the source of what is being said – is it coming from the spirit or is it coming from the soul. This gift, like conversion itself, is dependent on the hunger and thirst of the proponent for the will of God. If this gift is to be used in a worship service it should be no more than two or three at a time and this accompanied with *the gift of interpretation.*[235] Otherwise it it is for the speaker's own edification.

Prophecy is to be especially pursued.[236] Prophesy is defined as: *to foretell events, divine, speak under inspiration, exercise the prophetic office.*[237] It is not fortune telling it is speaking forth the word of God. This can be a direct auricular word, given thru' an individual, for any particular purpose at any particular time. If this is so it should be judged by others with a prophetic gift[238] and submitted to the Church oversight for directive action if necessary. Beware of someone who wants to give personal words unchecked by others, this can be very manipulative and should be avoided. Preaching should be under the inspiration of the Holy Spirit and therefore have a prophetic edge to it. Like all spiritual gifts there are different levels of operation. (1) *For you can all prophesy one by one;*[239] (2) The gift of prophesy;[240] (3) The prophetic office, those called out,[241] recognised by other prophets and church oversight.

New Testament prophecy is not the same as Old Testament prophecy. The Old Testament prophets were special individuals only. They spoke from the same Spirit but were called to temper the lives of kings and nations. In the New Testament, where the Spirit is given to all it is limited to *edification and exhortation and comfort to men.*[242] If judgemental and critical material comes forth this is not from God.

Discernment of spirits is another gift that can be exercised by those filled with the Spirit. It is different to the natural bent to assess people you meet. It is not just to discern the presence of evil spirits, tho' this may happen, it is given to discern the state of a person's soul and spirit with the aim of providing exhortation and/comfort for them.

The gift of healings (plural) is also available. Jesus did say most assuredly:*" he who believes in Me, the works that I do he will do also; and greater works than these he will do, because I go to My Father"*[243]. If these gifts are to be manifest it will require a great deal of prayer and waiting on the Holy Spirit to bring them to fruition but they are available to those hearing God's call; just so with *the gift of miracles.*

When *faith* arises to the gift level it brings forth many outcomes such as building projects and new ministry ventures etc.

The gift of a word of knowledge can often be used to reveal situations in a person's life or situation that can then receive ministry and edify the recipient. *The gift of a word of wisdom* can reveal ways of dealing with circumstances and situations that would not naturally be obvious.

GIFTS v MATURITY

Children may be very unwise with what they do with gifts given to them. It would be nice if maturity was given at the same time but it takes time to grow into. When the Holy Spirit arrives in a person's life at the time they are born again all of the resources of God are immediately available. Spiritual gifts are among them. There are two views as to how this happens.

1. When God originally designed a person He designed them with whatever spiritual gifts they needed just as they also received physical and mental gifts. When they are baptised in the Spirit, the Spirit enlivens those spiritual gifts within that were originally placed there.
2. When a person is baptised in the Spirit he/she, at that point, receives spiritual gifts from God. On subsequent occasions, by waiting on God, other gifts can be given.

What ever is the way, maturity and character development must take over. In the King James Version of the Bible the word perfection (Greek: *Telios*) is often used of a Christian seeking the ultimate in his/her walk with the Lord. Perfection is an unattainable goal. Anyone who managed to attain it would probably be directly translated to heaven; they would certainly be difficult to live with on earth. In many versions of scripture it is better rendered *mature*. It certainly also has the implication of *completeness*. There is a completeness of the giving of the grace, goodness and giftings of God but the maturity of life's operation needs the oversight of gifted pastors and those more experienced in the faith.

Baptism in the Holy Spirit can certainly supply an enthusiasm for the things of God but it needs to be balanced by study of the Word of God, prayer and continual obedience to what God is saying.

Chapter 14

MAKING JESUS LORD!

There is much argument these days about the name of God. Should the Scandinavian word "God" be used; should the Hebrew word "Yahweh" take its place? What about the Arab/Asian word "Allah," can it be used? The English word "Lord" is often used. Jesus got it wrong because he only used "Father." So much time is wasted on such trivialities when in life's reality there is little effort to personally and practically make Jesus king.

When people come to Christ there is usually great rejoicing and thanks for the salvation that has just been received. There should be just as much rejoicing about the fact that Jesus is now Lord of life!

DEMISE OF SELF NATURE

Jesus said: *Most assuredly, I say to you, unless a grain of wheat falls into the ground and dies, it remains alone; but if it dies, it produces much grain.*[244]

If we really want to see the Kingdom of God coming in power and reality then the King, in His kingdom of love, must be allowed to take his place at its head. Our experience in this fallen world allows too many choices about what we may want to do. If Jesus is to be Lord the choices must be narrowed in favour of what we know He wants. The choices that put what I want, first, must go.

Jesus gave us an explicit image of this in His submission to the Father's will. *"As the Father loved Me, I also have loved you; abide in My love. If you keep My commandments, you will abide in My love, just as I have kept My Father's commandments and abide in His love.*[245] Jesus kept this obedience in place all the way thru' both the physical and spiritual rigours of Calvary. It's not that he particularly wanted to go thru' this.. In the Garden of Gethsemane before the torturous event He was heard to say: *"O My Father, if it is possible, let this cup pass from Me; nevertheless, not as I will, but as You will."* [246]

Such sentiment is needed if we are to endure to the end[247] and actually help in establishing the eternal Kingdom of God.

OBEDIENCE IS THE KEY

We all hate being forced into obedience. This is why Jesus said: *If you love me, keep my commandments.*[248] If we can't tap into the loving relationship with Jesus then whatever we do to replicate the laws of the Bible will miss the mark in any societal cohesion (Church or state). The burgeoning divorce rate and the proliferation of penal institutions bear witness to this. Without the grace and love exhibited by Jesus we are stuck with an Old Testament law which everyone flouted.

The prophet Samuel got it right when he said: *"To obey is better than sacrifice."* It's not a matter of doing our ideas of good things we think God might like, it's being obedient to whatever is God's plan. Obedience is the key to God's continued presence in our life. Jesus said: *"If anyone loves Me, he will keep My word; and My Father will love him, and We will come to him and make Our home with him."*[249] Father, Son and Holy Spirit - all consciously available in the believer's life.

Many times people come to their Pastor asking questions like: "How can I know God's will for my life?" To begin to know the answer to a question like that there has to be a commitment to study God's Word with an undiminishing aspiration to do what it says plus an unreserved dependence on the abiding Spirit within. When God is convinced we mean it more specific leading will be forthcoming. Practical obedience to what we already know is a forerunner to finding out more.

POISE OF PRESENCE

Growing up in (and out) of a strongly conservative Church we were constantly bombarded with giving a good example to both the pagan world and our contemporises in the Church; *"be an example to the believers in word, in conduct, in love, in spirit, in faith, in purity."*[250] Nothing wrong with this, the Bible consistently puts this standard forward. But in some ways it is a negative of the positive side of enjoying the presence of God. If we are abiding in what we have of the Spirit of God we will automatically be that good example, it won't be hard at all.

If we are primarily concerned with maintaining the sense of the presence of God within and abiding in Christ then the love of God is always there. The pressure of a verse such as Luke 9: 23 *"If anyone desires to come after Me, let him deny himself, and take up his cross daily, and follow Me"* ceases. Self denial is no longer a problem. The cost of following Him is a delight not a trial because His presence is real.

When people wander into a church where the presence of God is evident there is an immediate rapport. Jesus is being exalted and lifted up as lord and king. Maintaining this 24/7 is the constant challenge. This is the cutting edge of the kingdom of God which the Spirit of God can use to build it.

In a usual secular situation the person in authority is grudgingly obeyed, harshness and punitive measures can often ensue. The "lord" is separate and rules from a distance. In the kingdom of God the "Lord" is with us every step of the way His love is ever there to help and encourage us. This love is there to often do it for us. His presence is there to discipline us and perfect us. His presence is always there for us.

He is only Lord because we invite Him into that position, He doesn't demand it. His presence is all the guarantee we need.

"IF HE IS NOT LORD OF ALL HE IS NOT LORD AT ALL."

Chapter 15

WHAT DOES JESUS WANT?

As much as Jesus is happy with us enjoying his presence within our own lives and sharing it with other Christians in church he sets before us an active role in his world-wide campaign to build the Kingdom of God.[251] He is insistent that this happens.[252] We were not translated into the Kingdom of heaven just to provide "fire insurance" to keep us out of Hell. We now share in the life goal of Jesus.

In the first three Gospels, Jesus lays out his **Great Commandment**: *You shall love the lord your God with all of your heart and soul and mind and your neighbour as yourself.* [253]

As Jesus was departing this world to go back to his Father he outlined, in brief, what we are to do with all that love – implement his **Great Commission** - *Mat 28:18-20. And Jesus came and spoke to them, saying, "All authority has been given to Me in heaven and on earth. Go therefore and make disciples of all the nations, baptizing them in the name of the Father and of the Son and of the Holy Spirit, teaching them to observe all things that I have commanded you; and lo, I am with you always, even to the end of the age." Amen.*

In no other place in the scriptures does Jesus so nakedly and blatantly demand his authority. It is not some arrogant outburst of a departing disillusioned saviour. It is an awesome invitation to join in the authority and power of the heavenly host to fulfil a destiny of godly love and peace forever. It arose from the willing worship offered by the fledgling Church.[254] The experience of functioning under the full power and authority of Jesus is more stirring than any other thing upon this earth. It involves dimensions of spiritual operation of incredible magnitude.

In spite of this what has actually happened is the **Great Omission:** in this twenty first century we have failed in the task.

The Great Commission is calling us to be true disciples of Jesus not just a cheer squad of people observing the great acts of saints recorded in the Bible or demonstrated now in our contemporary world. It is for men and women of faith, fulfilling whatever Jesus wants no matter how small the task.

Making disciples is not an option for Christians it is a command. Jesus said *"If you love Me, keep My commandments.*[255] It should come before any other thing happening in the church or the community. Disciple-making is a lost art for much of the world-wide church of the living God. It requires our loving response. It's what Jesus wants more than anything else.

The words of Matthew 28: 18 – 20 are the last thing the resurrected Jesus said before he went back to his Father. Surely he could have said anything else he thought most important for his disciples to do when he was gone. He could have talked about the Sermon on The Mount.[256] He could have stressed the importance of his parables.[257] He could have exegeted his second coming.[258] He did none of these things. He gave them the greatest task in the universe – go and make disciple makers.

WHAT IS A DISCIPLE?

According to the Concise Oxford Dictionary[259] a disciple is a *"follower, adherent, of any leader of thought, art, etc."* The dictionary uses Jesus 12 disciples as it's example.

Wherever Jesus went the disciples were sure to follow.
Whatever Jesus taught the disciples were sure to learn.
Whatever Jesus commanded the disciples were sure to obey.

The relationship of discipling that Jesus exercised was one such as a master and his apprentice would share. The discipling of a follower/labourer to the purposes of the master.

There is no room for rebellion in such a relationship. It is the loving, obedient regard of the follower/learner toward the father/teacher who is charged with the task of bringing the disciple to a place of maturity in the purposes of God. It is the process of bringing the disciple to the place where he/she can be personally led by the Spirit and now discipling others. It is not a place of permanent dependence on the discipler it is a place of dependence on the Holy Spirit.

Learning is something that goes on forever. No one can be a teacher without continuing to be a learner. The modern knowledge explosion warns us of that. In Hebrews chapter 5 the Holy Spirit is constrained to say: *For though by this time you ought to be teachers, you need someone to teach you again the first principles of the oracles of God; and you have come to need milk and not solid food. For everyone who partakes only of milk is unskilled in the word of righteousness, for he is a babe. But solid food belongs to those who are of full age, that is, those who by reason of use have their senses exercised to discern both good and evil.*[260]

Milk is something that has passed thru' someone else's digestive system (Eg the mother or the bottle). Solid food is something we have to work for, work at and ultimately enjoy the chewing labour. Milk is something that comes from the pastor, some TV programme, book or devotional source. Nothing wrong with milk, I still drink it, but it is not as important as the revelation God can give you personally from his word – that's meat, not milk !

DISCIPLING HAS THREE FUNDAMENTALS
– being, - imparting, - multiplying

Being is the milk stage of receiving from others. It is learning the basic tenants. This stage never ends because disciples are always required to learn. The process of being a disciple should result in the aspirant becoming self sufficient in prayer, handling the word of God truthfully, exercising spiritual gifts and generally fitting into his/her place in the Body of Christ.

Imparting is the place where the already received spiritual principle and practise is passed on to someone else. It is the place where the disciple has found trust in the heart of another who wants to receive in the same manner as the disciple himself has already completed.

This is not just a formal passing on of facts. It is teaching those *"who because of practise have their senses trained to discern."*[261]

Multiplying is the goal. It is the ultimate outworking of Jesus commission to *"teach them to observe all that I have commanded you."*[262] It is the disciple passing on that ability to another to make disciples themselves.

The foremost example of this pass-on-able principle is found in 2 Timothy 2: 2: *"And the things that you have heard from me among many witnesses, commit these to faithful men who will be able to teach others also."* Paul discipled Timothy; Timothy discipled *"faithful men;"* these in turn discipled *"others* [faithful men] *also."*[263] All of this_*"among many witnesses,"* that is, among the fellowship of many other Christians – Eg, the local church.

THE GREAT COMMISSION HAS FOUR STAGES

Jesus commanded disciples be made and left the initiative with the church –

1. ***It was for everyone:*** *"GO"* he said; 'do it,' don't sit around and wait for special mystical instructions, there won't be any, just go and get on with it.
2. ***It was universal:*** ... *"MAKE disciples of all nations."* Literally, *"make disciples of every ethnic group."*[264] Unfortunately many Christians are already to go off to some other continent or nation to make disciples when they have never done it where they are. With the current refugee situation and the concomitant movement of people groups across national borders there is ample evidence, of most any nation, in a reachable situation where you are now. It will be much harder in a strange culture and language. With a proven discipling ministry in the local church it will be possible to send out ethnic disciple makers back to their own nations.
3. ***It had a method:*** The only manner of disciple making given in Jesus great commission of Matthew 28: 19 is "... BAPTIZING THEM in the name of the Father, and of the Son, and of the Holy Spirit"

Baptism has been one of the most controversial doctrines of the Christian Church over its whole history and this passage is the key to it. But, since water is not mentioned in this text the sacrament of baptism will not be considered here.

Initially the disciple is called upon to be baptised in the name of the Father, that name is his authority. Here it carries the impetus of verse 18 when Jesus is announcing the totality of his authority.

The word *"baptise"* originally had the meaning *"to immerse."* This verse says a Christian is one who should be totally wrapped up (immersed) in the authority (name) of the Father, God.

The first principle of being a disciple is to understand the security of acceptance in the Father's family.

When you were born into your natural family you were completely under your father's authority and automatically became a full member of that family.[265] So it is in the Kingdom of God, when you were born anew into the Kingdom of God,[266] *baptised into the name of the Father,* you are incorporated into his family.

Many children, born into dysfunctional families, were mistakes, not intended or wanted in this world. There are no mistakes in the family of the Father. God saw you and loved you. He said *"I love you and I want you to be a part of my family."* No mistakes about this. God says: *"I have a choice. I'm adopting you purely and simply because I love you and can't do without you. You are secure in my relationship with you. No one can take you out of my bosom.*[267] *I paid for you with the blood of your brother – enjoy being with me." "For you did not receive the spirit of bondage again to fear, but you received the Spirit of adoption by whom we cry out, 'Abba, Father'."*[268]

As this verse says, bondage and fear are not part of the father/ child relationship in the family of God. Rather, the loving, respectful, familiarity of personal intimacy that enables a disciple to call the Father *"abba"* – my very own dad. All this brought about by the Holy Spirit within. *For as many as are led by the Spirit of God, these are sons of God.*[269]

It is wonderful to enjoy the security of a family whose Father provides, protects and gives secure direction for the future. This has nothing to do with a doctrine to fill up our brains – it is a real relationship with the real creator and sustainer of the universe.

The second principle is understanding inheritance.

To be *baptised into the name of the Son* means to be completely aware of the rights, privileges and responsibilities you share with Jesus. *"The Spirit Himself bears witness with our spirit that we are children of God, and if children, then heirs—heirs of God and joint heirs with Christ, if indeed we suffer with Him, that we may also be glorified together."*[270]

Since the Father will never die He has given everything to the Son already. The ability to claim the promises of God from the word of God; to find answers to prayer that are beyond the normal realms of possibility; to share with others the love and life of Jesus; to enjoy the presence and ministrations of the Holy Spirit are just some of the inheritance of the Kingdom of God in which you participate. They have to do with life not things.

"And for this reason He (Jesus) *is the Mediator of the new covenant, by means of death, ... that those who are called may receive the promise of the eternal inheritance. For where there is a testament, there must also of necessity be the death of the testator. For a testament is in force after men are dead, since it has no power at all while the testator lives."* [271]

The worldly death of our elder brother leads us to glorification and ultimate life in the heavenly places (now).

A friend[272] had this cute little song he would often sing:

> *"My Father owns the heavens,*
> *My Father owns the earth,*
> *I'm his child and I'm his heir,*
> *I just don't know how much I'm worth.*

We may enjoy the thought of all the gracious things God is making available to us but it all comes at a price and not just the incredible price paid at Calvary, we can't enter into that. But, firstly, we can accept the *responsibility* of looking after the things bequeathed to us. Failing to act on this means we will lose what we gained and our witness will suffer, to say nothing of the abiding presence within. Secondly, *"we suffer with him"* as we tap into his heart, sensing the pain that he feels as he agonizes over the lost-ness of mankind in its sin and selfishness.

It is the lifelong task of every disciple to appropriate all of the promises and responsibilities associated with Jesus heritage.

The third principle is Empowerment

To be *baptised in the Holy Spirit* means to be immersed in the personal facilitation of God thru' the indwelling ministry of the Holy

Spirit. Everywhere baptism of the Spirit is mentioned in the scripture there is ample, obvious, evidence of the miraculous operation of the Holy Spirit.

"But if the Spirit of Him who raised Jesus from the dead dwells in you, He who raised Christ from the dead will also give life to your mortal bodies through His Spirit who dwells in you."[273]

Here is our personal power to bring into being all of the attitudes spoken of above. If all of the principles mentioned above are only letters of the law then we are in for a tough time and so are the people to whom we bear witness. Being 'hit over the head' by heavy bible verses, no matter how true, is very likely to cause brain damage. On the contrary, if these same verses are infused into another's spirit by the loving Holy Spirit, a new life begins to inhabit the Kingdom of God.

The fourth principle is continuous reproduction.

"TEACHING THEM TO OBSERVE ALL THAT I HAVE COMMANDED THEM"

The job is not finished after a person has been baptised it's only just started. Obviously Jesus must have taught his disciples how to teach others to teach others how to make disciples. If he hadn't done this Christianity would have ended after the next generation.

We all need a structured way to make disciple-makers. If we don't have this it can be assured we will not be making disciples let alone those who can make other disciples. Our plan may have to be flexible enough to cope with the all the vagaries of human experience but it must have certain goals – how to pray, how to meditate on the word of God, how to abide in Christ, how to develop gifts, how to fit into the Church, how to witness, how to obediently make Jesus lord of life, how to draw on the power of the Holy Spirit, plus anything you have found helpful in being the example of a disciple that pleases Jesus.

Telling isn't teaching and listening isn't learning. In the process of establishing a disciple there must be ample play-back time and opportunities to check that what is being taught has to become a part of the new disciple. This requires work; this will be in vain if the aspirant is not faithful. But if he/she is faithful this will be the most rewarding thing you will ever do.

QUALITY BRINGS QUANTITY

It's so important that Christians undergo a quality check. The type of disciple Jesus wanted left so much responsibility resting on them.

"For the earnest expectation of the creation eagerly waits for the revealing of the sons of God. For the creation was subjected to futility, not willingly, but because of Him who subjected it in hope; because the creation itself also will be delivered from the bondage of corruption into the glorious liberty of the children of God."[274]

When the children of God become the disciples they were supposed to be; when they are the visible "baptised" children of God they will release this world from its bondage and suffering. That is the promise of God.

What an exciting destiny for disciples of Christ - surely the most important thing in the world.

It is so easy to get involved in the church. We can be so extended fulfilling a variety of tasks when all the time Jesus is calling us to be 'makers of disciple makers.'

The Apostle Paul understood the importance of the disciple making task. When writing to the Church in Colossae he enthusiastically speaks of:*"Christ in you, the hope of glory. Him we proclaim, warning every man and teaching every man in all wisdom, that we may present every man mature in Christ. For this I toil striving with all the energy which he mightily inspires within me."*[275]

Chapter 16

DISCIPLING FOR DESTINY

We have a stark choice in life! Are we going to be involved in the directing of lives on into eternity or are we going to be mere uninvolved spectators in the passing parade of time?

For the Christian the choice is already made. Jesus tells us we must be reproducers of our kind – real disciples!

When a person first enters the Church of the living God and looks around at those already there, they tend to become like those they are now associating with. If the norm of those with whom they are becoming familiar is to sit on a church pew once a Sunday then that is exactly what the new "Christian" will also do. If what they see is the same as that which is described in the Bible then they will become true disciples of Jesus Christ like those around them.

The Twentieth and Twenty First Centuries have produced an awesome number of mega-churches and mammoth religious organizations. In reaction to this many commentators have branded big as "bad" and have opted for small churches or house groups as the way to go. Reaction seldom produces righteousness. Neither big nor small is the answer. To look merely on externals such as size can really miss the mark. *"Jesus said ... My food (nourishment) is to do the will (pleasure) of Him who sent Me and to accomplish and completely finish His work."*[276]

Someone once commented that anyone could build a large religious organization, all they had to do was work hard at whatever it was they wanted to do whether it be a large church or multi-element organization.

This says little for the diligence of many ministers and even less for the quality of commitment of average churchgoers. The "success" of twentieth first century cults is appalling testimony to the accuracy of these claims.

Many religious organizations would look to the Bible for rationale to justify their existence. Just because Bible verses are quoted does not mean that truth is being propounded. Even the devil used Bible verses when he had Jesus on the ropes in their battle in the desert shortly after Jesus baptism[277]. It was Jesus superior knowledge of the Scripture[278] and the ever-present power of the Holy Spirit[279] that brought victory over the devil and his wiles. It will be the same for us.

In our quest for truth it must be to the Bible that we go. It must be to a consistent interpretation that stands the test of time and of Jesus own personality. *"Jesus Christ is the same yesterday and today, yes and forever. Do not be carried away by varied and strange teachings; for it is good for the heart to be strengthened ["established" - KJV] by grace."*[280] If what is being taught and espoused is not the same as has consistently been taught throughout the ages then there is ample grounds for rejecting that which is being offered (or in other cases that which is being forced down the throat). The consistency of Biblical doctrine and its resolute historic reinforcement throughout the ages, together with the unction of the Holy Spirit is the only stable basis for true discipleship.

The familiar words of Matthew 28:18-20 are the springboard that launches us into a discipling ministry.

A disciple is one who is self sufficient in his relationship with God. One who is able to hear from God for himself, handle the word of God confidently, able to discern the will of God for his own direction in life, is submissive to the authority placed over him in the corporate affairs of the Church and thereby able to exercise the authority invested in him by the Holy Spirit and the Church oversight. He is one who is able to reproduce after his own kind.

The destiny of this world is tied up in the disciple making ability of the Church of the Living God.

OUTCOMES EXPECTED OF A DISCIPLE

You will know you have produced a true disciple when: -

They are self motivated feeding themselves as evidenced by spending time every day in prayer and Bible study, willingly and obediently hearing from the Spirit of God.

They are abiding in Christ: Turning to Jesus immediately when under pressure, being in a place of trust and rest rather than stress, fear or worry.

They have truly made Jesus Lord as evidenced by a willingness to obey and follow where the Holy Spirit leads and by being selfless and sacrificial in the service of others.

They are committed to the local Church shown by regular attendance and involvement with love for other believers and the ability to relate in healthy empowering ways.

They have a genuine concern for the lost which means they truly understand the Gospel and are sharing their faith, inviting people to Church.

They have a hunger to be Christ-like as evidenced by a desire to grow in maturity as a Christian with personal holiness and a God honouring lifestyle.

They see the people they minister to reproducing after their own kind.

HELP FROM THE SPIRIT OF GOD

Before we become overwhelmed by the expectation and responsibilities of the task detailed above we need to realize that we are not alone in this awesome task. We have someone far more interested in its outcome than we are – the Holy Spirit. We must also recognize that help can also come from mutual sharing in the Body of Christ – the Church.

Becoming the full blown archetypal disciple is not going to happen overnight it is a learning process which may mean learning from some mistakes along the way.

For by grace you have been saved through faith, and that not of yourselves; it is the gift of God,[281] There is a liberty in the grace of God that releases us from the tension and responsibility of achievement. If our attitude is right the grace of God smoothes our way and enables us to enjoy the ride and fulfil the destiny.

The Baptism of the Holy Spirit employs in us the best help available. Learning to draw on this, releases in us the personal power of our Father to accomplish any task he sets before us. The Spirit's best work of revealing Jesus comes from here.

THE POWER OF THE PRESENCE

Chapter 14 drew attention to the fact that Jesus last words came to the disciples as they were worshipping.[251] A Church that really worships in Spirit will draw people to Jesus. From here they can be discipled to the masters loving desires.

Worship is not a mind game! It's not a matter of just putting together God words, ensuring they are correct, getting them in our eyes and then out of our mouths. It is also not a culture-conforming exercise. - "This is the disciplined way we do things - do what everyone else is doing – the way we have always done it." Discipline is certainly a desirable fruit of the spirit[252] but it should not be used to stultify the creative flow of the Spirit in worship by conforming.

Worship is something of the reality (truth) of the Spirit. "*Where the Spirit is there is liberty.*"[282] There must be room for the creative energy of the Spirit to move true worshippers in whatever way they together (Holy Spirit and worshipper) want to go. Praise brings the presence of the Lord; worship indulges it. The strength of worship is a drawing power to the Church.

The presence of God is what we are aiming at when we arrive in heaven, there is no reason why we can't have a bit of it now and bring some heaven down to earth.

It was the fact that the disciples were worshipping in Matthew 28: 17 that drew Jesus to give his Great Commission at that point in time. When worship in the Spirit is happening it prepares the human heart to receive revelation from the Word of God. It can empower personal evangelism, disciple making or anything else God may want. The early disciples went out with exuberant, loving hearts – they were irresistible. They met persecution with love before apology (spirit before brain) an example to our 21st century media and scientific persecutors.

Chapter 17

THE IMMEDIATE RESULT OF JESUS WORDS

THE "BREATH OF GOD"

On Sunday, the same day of Jesus resurrection, He lost no time in appearing to His disciples.[283] He had already given them His Great Commission – what was left to say and do with them now?

First he gave them a précis of the Commission: *So Jesus said to them again, "Peace to you! As the Father has sent Me, I also send you."*[284]

Next he restyled his teaching about the Paraclete from John 14 – 16. *And when He had said this, He breathed on them, and said to them, "Receive the Holy Spirit.*[285]

Now He focused on the single-most gain of the coming kingdom which He had just so adequately demonstrated – forgiveness. *If you forgive the sins of any, they are forgiven them; if you retain the sins of any, they are retained."*[286]

Here is the progression: Jesus is resurrected. >He quickly talks to His disciples. >He commissions them again > He releases the Holy Spirit to them to empower the directive >He immediately ties forgiveness to this. He had already extensively taught on this previously in Matthew 18 highlighting what John also recorded in Matthew 16: 19 and 18: 18.

It would be wonderful to think that Church and Christian fellowship would be a place where there would never be offence. Unfortunately this is so idealistic it is an offence in itself. Jesus said *"It is impossible that no offences should come."*[287] While Jesus is scathing about those who bring offence He is also telling us to grow up and learn how to deal with them

Forgiveness is the whole key to the Gospel. Jesus forgave and tells us to do the same. *"Father, forgive them, for they do not know what they do."*[288] When Jesus forgives that's it. No more recriminations, no more digging up the past. No more gossip; no more living in the gloom of past wrongs. Jesus forgot about the past. Instead, gave all his life intention to sharing the love of God, worshipping Him and redeeming mankind. No more bondage to the past.

But if the Spirit of Him who raised Jesus from the dead dwells in you, He who raised Christ from the dead will also give life to your mortal bodies through His Spirit who dwells in you.[289]

The sad fact is there are so many so called Christians who see themselves as having been hurt by other Christians. Say they have forgiven the ones who they see as responsible, but still live in the "hurt." This is bondage! *"Assuredly, I say to you, whatever you bind on earth will be bound in heaven, and whatever you loose on earth will be loosed in heaven.*[290] Scratch these people and the hurt will soon come up. When discussing other Christian situations, out it will quickly come. This means they have never died to themselves. The corn of wheat never fell into the ground and died,[291] instead, self on the throne needed some reason why it could justify not achieving its desired status. It was all other peoples fault. The apostle Paul "died daily"[292] to make sure he wasn't bound by any of the wrongs done to him. *For whoever desires to save his life will lose it, but whoever loses his life for My sake and the gospel's will save it.*[293]

Unless we can expel these hurts we become useless in the Kingdom of God no matter how much we say we believe in Jesus. Forgiveness is complete, not something we dredge up whenever we feel sorry for ourselves or want to justify our own selfish actions (or non-actions).

Remember Naaman, the Syrian General who went to see the Prophet Elisha to be healed of his leprosy.[294] When the Prophet didn't even come out to see him but sent a servant to tell him to dip himself in the mud pot Jordan seven times, he got offended. While he stayed offended he got nothing from God. When he came to terms with the request and humbled himself, God healed him.

Lack of full forgiveness is the biggest problem with the full release of the Spirit. It is also a salient reason why we don't pray enough. We won't see much of the presence and power of God if we don't forgive. Every time we come to talk to God it won't be long before this comes up, either consciously or unconsciously, blocking the way for Jesus to answer positively and reducing the rapport we have with the Father.

THE RELEASE OF THE SPIRIT

The breath of God is for every Christian – we need to take full advantage and be released into God's fullness and serve Him – His way, blessing those who have despitefully used us.

Then He said to them, *"Thus it is written, and thus it was necessary for the Christ to suffer and to rise from the dead the third day, and that repentance and remission of sins should be preached in His name to all nations, beginning at Jerusalem. And you are witnesses of these things. Behold, I send the Promise of My Father upon you; but tarry in the city of Jerusalem until you are endued with power from on high."*[295]

So the disciples waited. By twenty first century standards this must have been an excruciating period, this generation has trouble waiting for anything. We all want instant gratification.

God has plenty of time in fact He has an eternity. Waiting on God's Spirit is a discipline we all need to learn. The disciples filled this time of waiting with prayer.[296] What they were waiting for they didn't know. They only knew Jesus had told them to do it. When the day of Pentecost came and the Holy Spirit made such a mess they hung on to the Spirit in the midst of it and miracles followed.

And it wasn't for just a day!

The Gospel of Mark records the response: *And these signs will follow those who believe: In My name they will cast out demons; they will speak with new tongues; they will take up serpents; and if they drink anything deadly, it will by no means hurt them; they will lay hands on the sick, and they will recover."*[297] The disciples took the Master at his word. *And they went out and preached everywhere, the Lord working with them and confirming the word through the accompanying signs. Amen.*[298]

If we do the "waiting" we will likely see the miracles!

ACTION STRATEGY

These early disciples, taking in the Word of God daily, continually developing regular prayer habits, consistently obedient, responsively empowered by the Holy Spirit,[299] *"went everywhere preaching the word."*[300] They were incredibly successful. It was said of the Romans that their faith was *"spoken of throughout the whole world"*[301] and of the Thessalonians, that *"from you sounded out the Word of the Lord ... in every place."*[302] History tells us that the Apostle Thomas reached China with the gospel; Churches in India still bear his name.[303] From Phillip's preaching in Acts 8 it went into Africa, still evidenced by the Coptic Churches in Ethiopia, Egypt and other places. British Churches were represented at a Church Conference in the early second century, and so on.

What brought about such growth?

Answer: Real Spirit empowered communication of the Gospel plus consistent discipling of new believers who themselves discipled others. New Christians were helped to *"grow in grace."*[304]

What killed such growth?

The life Jesus promised[305] was in the Church, many people came and enjoyed it but there was no spiritual calling in them. Gradually the weight of numbers of such people combined with the official acceptance of the Roman Empire just made it another religion and the power departed. It became a dry formal creed.

It doesn't have to be like that. This was not what Jesus intended. The breath of God is still available to release the Spirit into action.

WHERE TO NOW?

At various points in history since that first falling back there have been those who have heard the calling of God and when enough of these people have come together in one place with real hunger and thirst for Jesus, revival has broken out. People have come to Christ in large numbers, Christians have reconsecrated and have become sound fruit-bearing disciples and Churches have grown with new Churches being planted.

We often talk and preach about the Anointing of the Holy Spirit. We have usually defined the anointing as "the focused presence of God for a particular purpose of God." We have also seen in 1 John 2: 27 that, for the Christian, anointing is associated with the state of "abiding." It logically follows then the focused presence of God should continually live within the Christian. In other words it should not just be an event or sensation on a special occasion it should be that same special spiritual sensitivity and power, living on the inside all the time. This was certainly true for Jesus; His title, Christ, literally means 'The Anointed One.'

It becomes very important that we learn to live in the manifested anointing of the Holy Spirit. Remember: the Spirit is Holy. If we are going to have Him continually gracing our lives in power and strength we had better decide very quickly that we are going to live in a very holy manner. If not we will soon find that the anointing, as already defined above, is no longer there. Jesus may be living in our lives but we can forget any anointing! This means we can forget any healing, power or sense of His presence. In other words if we are not prepared to give up our gossip, sensuality and un-separated worldly living, how is a holy God going to anoint us? He is certainly not going to anoint our television sets instead of our prayer closets.

When we do decide to do it God's way then we can claim the anointed promises of Ps. 92:10-15. *He will cause us to:-*

1. *See* our victory (v.11a).
2. *Hear* what the devil's plotting against us (v.11b).
3. *Flourish* (v.12a).
4. *Grow* (v.12b).
5. *Be established in the blessing* (v.13).
6. *Be fruitful* (v.14).
7. *Show the Lord to the world* (v.15).

Altogether - see the Kingdom of God grow before our eyes.

EPILOGUE

The probing enigma of the New Testament is *"The dynamic interaction between the Holy Spirit, the Body of Christ and the Word of God"*[306] and this translated into the continuum of the local Church. This work (and many others), tell us that these three things (Word, Body and Spirit) must work together to round-out the ongoing life of the believer. If any one of these loses its inherent vibrancy not much will happen in the believer's life. The true dynamic is the integration of all three.

It's exciting to discover for your self the timeless doctrines of the scripture but the dynamic comes as we search out what we have discovered from The Word, and allow the power of the Holy Spirit to confirm their veracity in the orthodoxy of the Body of Christ. The result should appear practically in the world around us.

Correctly engaging prayer with The Word in the fellowship of a lively Body of Christ should produce abundant fruit in the life of any believer.

Many Churches have large bodies of older people in their congregations, convinced they can now take it easy after a lifetime of work and service, the goal of life now disentangled from the aspirations of the Church Nothing could be further from the truth! Psalm 92 points out *"Those who are planted in the house of the LORD Shall flourish in the courts of our God. They shall still bear fruit in old age; They shall be fresh and flourishing,"*[307] No matter what age we are, young or old, God still has a purpose for us in His great kingdom. Embrace it and enjoy the fruit!

ENDNOTES

Introduction
1 James 5: 19 - 20

Chapter 1 Finding "The Way."
2 Before believers in Christ were first called Christians (Acts 9: 26), they were known as "The Way" (Acts 9: 2).
3 Church Growth 1 notes, Prof. C. Peter Wagner, page 1074.
4 © The Sentinel Group

Chapter 2 Early Along "The Way."
5 Ephesians 4: 20
6 Jeremiah 29: 11
7 2 Corinthians 3: 18
8 "Hazarding the Risks" by David Allan Hubbard. "Signs & Wonders Today" Edited by C. Peter Wagner; © 1987 by C. Peter Wagner (Creation House, Strang Communications Company, 190 Westmonte Drive Alamonte Springs FL 32714), Page 15.
9 2 Corinthians 3: 18
10 Proverbs 4 : 23
11 Eg. 1 Corinthians 12: 4 – 10; Romans 12: 4 – 8; Ephesians 4: 11; et al.

Chapter 3 The God Who Never Gives Up
12 Deuteronomy 23: 5; John 16: 23
13 John 15: 8 – 11
14 © 2000; Quin Sherrer and Ruthanne Garlock; "Praying Prodigals Home"

(Regal, A Division of Gospel Light, Ventura California USA) Foreword.

15 © 1996 Dutch Sheets : "Intercessory Prayer:" (Regal, a Division of Gospel Light, Ventura California USA)

16 John 13: 35 →18: 16, 25, 27

17 Colossians 4: 10

18 Acts 12: 25

19 Acts 13: 13

20 Acts 13: 37

21 Colossians 4: 10 & 11; 2 Timothy 4: 11; Philemon 24

22 1 Peter 5: 13

23 The Maxwell Leadership Bible ©2002 by Maxwell Motivation Inc. Page 1186./ Dake's Annotated Reference Bible by Finis Jennings Dake, Dake Publishing, Inc. PO Box 1050 Lawrenceville, Georgia 30046, Large Print Edition © 1999 Eleventh printing – March 2013.

24 Colossians 4: 14

25 2 Timothy 4: 10

26 Philemon 24

27 Strongs Hebrew & Greek Dictionaries per E-sword.

28 Verse 19

Chapter 4 Review

29 Ephesians 2: 8 - 9

30 Acts 2: 37 (Amp)

31 Acts 11: 18

32 2 Timothy 2: 25

33 Romans 2: 4

34 Philippians 2: 5

35 Romans 15: 6; 2 Corinthians 8: 12

36 2 Corinthians 7: 9 & 10

37 1 Thessalonians 1: 9 & 10

38 Luke 5: 32

39 Acts 20: 21

40 Acts 3: 19

41 Luke 5: 32

42 1 Corinthians 15: 1 – 8

43 The Amplified Bible, Expanded Edition, Copyright © 1987 by the Zondervan Corporation and the Lockman Foundation; Preface vi.

44 Matthew 6: 33

45 John 1: 12 & 13
46 John 14: 21
47 Hebrews 11: 6
48 John 20: 22 – 23
49 Luke 24: 45 – 47 [Amp]
50 Luke 6: 37
51 Luke 11: 4
52 1Peter 3: 21

Chapter 5 Living In The Kingdom

53 John 15: 4
54 John 15
55 Galatians 5: 25
56 Galatians 2: 20
57 Philippians 1: 21
58 Isaiah 40: 11
59 Exodus 33: 14
60 "Abiding in Christ," Mark Virkler (Peacemakers Newsletter No 25, 1996; Peacemakers PO Box 600 Cootamundra N.S.W.2590) Page 3.
61 John 15: 5
62 John 15: 2
63 John 15: 6
64 John 15: 9; 3: 16
65 1 John 1: 9
66 Exodus 33: 14
67 Hebrews 4: 1
68 Jeremiah 29: 11
69 Joshua 1: 8
70 John 8: 31, 32
71 Matthew 13: 34
72 Matthew 13: 13ff

Chapter 6 Developing Relationship

73 Robert Foster: Tract, "Time Alone With God" © Navigators (Sydney, Christchurch)
74 Genesis 19: 27
75 Exodus 34: 4
76 Daniel 6: 10

77 Mark 1: 35

78 Acts 5: 21

79 Matthew 6: 33

80 Psalm 5: 3

81 "The Quiet Time, "Gibbs Alfred P. (Good News Publishers, Westchester, Ill), page 4.

Chapter 7 Empowering Relationship

82 2Samuel 22: 7 & 18

83 Psalm 62: 8

84 Times Square Church Pulpit Series.

85 2Samuel 22: 2 - 4

86 Ibid

87 Baker Book House, Grand Rapids, Michigan (1980).

88 Isaiah 26: 9 (NIV)

89 Psalm 100: 1 – 5

90 Psalm 57: 8

91 Psalm 59: 16

92 1Thessalonians 5: 18

93 Verses 1 – 3

94 Morgan & Scott, London

95 Just So Stories (1902) 'The Elephants Child'

96 Psalm 119: 97, 100 & 152 NIV

97 Lamentations 3: 22 & 23

Chapter 8 Understanding Relationship

98 "Prayer" by O. Hallesby, translated by C. J. Carlsen (London, Inter-Varsity Fellowship, 1965 edition) Page 9.

99 "Master Secrets of Prayer" by Cameron V. Thompson (© 1959 by Good News Broadcasting Association Inc.) Pages 10 – 11.

100 Proverbs 8: 34 - 35

101 Romans 8: 26

102 "The Power Factor," George and Meg Patterson [© Word (UK) Edition 1986] Page 85.

103 Matthew 6: 9 – 13; Luke 11: 2 - 4

104 Fuller Theological Seminary, Church Growth 1 Notes (1986), Prof C Peter Wagner; Church Growth Pathology, Page 14.

105 Matthew 6; 8

106 1Thessalonians 5: 18; Romans 8: 18
107 1John 5: 14
108 Romans 8: 29

Chapter 9 Enlisting The Word

109 Joshua 1: 8
110 Jeremiah 15: 16
111 Psalm 1: 1 - 3
112 James 1: 21b
113 James 1: 25
114 Hebrews 5: 12 - 14
115 Psalm 65: 5 and 6
116 Psalm 119: 97
117 Colossians 3: 16
118 Proverbs 6: 22 & 23
119 1 Corinthians 10: 19 & 20
120 Romans 12: 1; Philippians 2: 5
121 Psalm 77: 6
122 1Corinthians 2: 9
123 1Corinthians 2: 10
124 Romans 8: 27

Chapter 10 More Word

125 James 1: 21 (Amp)
126 KJV
127 James 1: 22
128 Matthew 5: 6
129 Hosea 10: 12
130 Psalm 119: 11
131 Proverbs 4: 23
132 Deuteronomy 6: 6
133 Colossians 3: 16a
134 Matthew 4: 4
135 1Peter 2: 2
136 Hebrews 4: 12
137 Mark 4: 19 (NIV)
138 Hebrews 4: 12
139 Jeremiah 15: 16

140 Psalm 119: 11

Chapter 11 Widening Relationship

141 Mark 12: 29 – 31 (Matthew 22: 37; Mark 12: 30)

142 Matthew 16: 18

143 Matthew 18: 21 - 35

144 The Maxwell Leadership Bible Copyright© 2002 by Maxwell Motivation, Inc. Page 1433.

145 Hebrews 13: 17

146 1John 1: 1 - 4

147 I n a sermon delivered at Scot's church, Sydney.

148 Ephesians 4: 16

149 Ephesians 4: 12 & 13

150 Hebrews 7: 28

151 John 4: 23 & 24

152 Matthew 20: 26-28

153 Matthew 23: 11 & 12

154 John 12: 26

155 Galatians 5: 13

156 John 13: 34 & 35

157 Mark 9: 35

158 John 16: 13 & 14

159 Hebrews 1: 9

160 Ephesians 4: 1 – 7

161 Matthew 5: 9

Chapter 12 The Paraclete

162 This montage about Jesus is by personal courtesy of Pastor Brian Bernays

163 John 20: 22

164 John 16: 14

165 Jesus uses the Greek word "allos" = another of the same kind ... one just like Me. He will do in My absence what I would do If I were physically present with you. The Spirit's coming assures continuity with what Jesus did and taught. – Word Wealth, Spirit-Filled Life Bible, page 1603, © 1991 by Thomas Nelson Inc

166 Different Bible versions use any one of these words to translate Parakletos.

167 Ezekiel 37: 14

168 Jeremiah 31: 33

169 Joel 2: 28

170 Matthew 3: 11; Mark 1: 7; Luke 3: 16.

171 John 7: 37 - 39

172 Numbers 20: 10

173 John 14: 15 - 16

174 John 14: 17

175 John 14: 18

176 John 14: 26

177 See also "Walking on the Inside" © 2015 by Dr Colin Crago (published by Tate Publishing and Enterprises, LLC, Mustang, Oklahoma, USA.)

178 John 16: 7

179 John 16: 8 - 11

180 Romans 5: 7

181 Galatians 5: 22 - 23

182 Acts 1: 8

Chapter 13 The Power

183 "THE HOLY SPIRIT Activating God's Power in Your Life" © 1978 by Billy Graham (William Collins Sons & Co Ltd London Glasgow Sydney Auckland Toronto Johannesburg) Selections from Introduction: Man's Cry – God's Gift, page 11.

184 Micah 6: 8

185 Romans 2: 4

186 Acts 1: 8a

187 Eg. Nicodemus - John 3: 1 - 8

188 Eg. The Apostle John - John 20: 22

189 Matthew 3: 11

190 Acts 1: 4b - 5

191 Acts 2: 1a

192 Acts 17: 6

193 Acts 2: 32-33

194 Acts 2: 39

195 Acts 1: 15

196 Acts 2: 1 - 13

197 Acts 1: 14

198 Acts 1: 5

199 Verse 1

200 Verse 2

201 Verse 3

202 Verse 4

203 Verse 12

204 Verse 13

205 Verse 15

206 Joel 2: 27 - 29

207 Joel 2:30 - 31

208 Acts 2: 41

209 Acts 4: 4

210 Usually there are many more women than men in religious meetings.

211 Acts 1: 8

212 Acts 6: 5

213 Acts 8: 5

214 Acts 8: 6 - 8

215 Acts 8: 16

216 Acts 8: 14 - 17

217 Acts 8: 9-11; 13; 18 – 24. Simon the sorcerer has been attributed by some as one of the founders of the early Christian heresy "Gnosticism" (salvation by knowledge).

218 Acts 10: 1 – 34; 11: 1 - 14

219 Acts 10: 34 – 44

220 Acts 11: 15 - 17

221 Acts 11: 18

222 Acts 13: 4

223 Acts 13: 1 - 2

224 Verse 1

225 Verse 2a

226 Verse 2b - 3

227 Verses 4 - 6

228 1 Corinthians 14: 1

229 There are two main Greek words used in the New Testament translated as "gift." Strong's Dictionary gives them as (1) Dorea = gift, gratuity and (2) Charismata = specifically a (spiritual) endowment, (objectively) miraculous faculty:- free gift.

230 1Corinthians 14: 2

231 1 Corinthians 14: 4

232 Titus 3: 2

233 1 Corinthians 14: 27 - 28

234 1 Corinthians 14: 1

235 Strong's dictionary

236 1 Corinthians 14: 29
237 1 Corinthians 14: 31
238 1 Corinthians 12: 10
239 Ephesians 4: 11
240 1 Corinthians 14: 3
241 John 14: 12

Chapter 14 Making Jesus Lord
242 John 12: 24
243 John 15: 9 - 10
244 Matthew 26: 39
245 Matthew 10: 22
246 John 15: 14
247 John 14: 23
248 1Timothy 4: 12 et al.

Chapter 15 What Does Jesus Want?
249 Kingdom of Heaven used mostly in Matthew's Gospel & Kingdom of God used mostly in Luke's Gospel, they are one & the same.
250 Mark 16: 15 – 20; Luke 24: 45 – 48.
251 Matthew 22: 37; Mark 12: 30; Luke 10: 27; this is not a direct quote it is a blend of the 3 verses.
252 Matthew 28: 17
253 John 14:15
254 Matthew 5 - 7
255 Matthew 13
256 Matthew 24: Luke 21.
257 Oxford University Press, London. 1960; page 341.
258 Verses 12 - 14
259 Hebrews 5: 14
260 Matthew 28: 20
261 The original language carried the idea of "others of the same sort."
262 Greek "ta ethne" = all ethnics, or every tongue tribe & nation.
263 If you were born into a single parent family there is still no doubt about family relationship.
264 John 3: 3 - 8
265 Hebrews 13: 5
266 Romans 8: 15

267 Romans 8: 14
268 Romans 8: 16 & 17
269 Hebrews 9: 15 - 17
270 Billie McAlpin
271 Romans 8: 11
272 Romans 8: 19 - 21
273 Colossians 1: 27 – 29 RSV.

Chapter 16 Discipling for Destiny

274 John 4: 34 (Amp)
275 Matthew 4: 6
276 Matthew 4: 4, 7, 10
277 Matthew 4: 1
278 Hebrews 13: 8, 9 (NIV)
279 Ephesians 2: 8
280 Matthew 28: 17
281 Galatians 5: 23
282 2Corinthians 3: 17

Chapter 17 The Immediate Result of Jesus Words

283 John 20: 19 – 24 (minus Thomas)
284 John 20: 21
285 John 20: 22
286 John 20: 23
287 Luke 17: 1
288 Luke 23: 34
289 Romans 8: 11
290 Matthew 18: 18
291 John 12: 24
292 1Corinthians 15: 31
293 Mark 8: 35
294 2Kings 5: 1 - 18
295 Luke 24: 46 – 49; Acts 1: 8
296 Acts 1: 4 – 5; 12 – 14
297 Mark 16: 17 – 18
298 Mark 16: 20
299 Acts 2: 42
300 Acts 8: 4

301 Romans 1: 8
302 1Thessalonians 1: 8
303 *Mar Thoma*, meaning "from Thomas."
304 2Peter 3: 18
305 John 14: 6

Epilogue

306 "The Pentecostal Commentary|New Testament; Editors Preface, John Christopher Thomas PhD (© 2004 T & T CLARK INTERNATIONAL *A Continum imprint* London – New York) Page *x*.
307 Verses 13 - 14

The inward man is being renewed day by day
2 Corinthians 4: 16

·ion can be obtained
·.com

⌐0004B/39/P

9 781984 504890